975
SOU

The South for new
southerners.

$22.50   923079

97

The South for New Southerners

T H E

South

F O R

New Southerners

Edited by Paul D. Escott & David R. Goldfield

The University of North Carolina Press ✪ Chapel Hill & London

The paper in this book meets the guidelines for permanence and
durability of the Committee on Production Guidelines for Book
Longevity of the Council on Library Resources.

Manufactured in the United States of America

95 94 93 92 91 5 4 3 2 1

Library of Congress Cataloging-in-Publication Data

The South for new southerners / edited by Paul D. Escott and
David R. Goldfield.

p. cm.

Includes bibliographical references and index.

ISBN 0-8078-1932-8 (cloth : alk. paper).—

ISBN 0-8078-4293-1 (pbk. : alk. paper)

1. Southern States—Civilization.   I. Escott, Paul D., 1947–
II. Goldfield, David R., 1944–

F209.S7   1991

975—dc20   90-50015

CIP   AAC 6186

For Southerners Present and Future

CONTENTS

Getting to Know the South

PAUL D. ESCOTT

The South is one of America's special regions—special in its history, its character, its ways of life, and the good life it has to offer. Newcomers may feel puzzled or perplexed by the differences they encounter, but that is not unusual. A little frustration or even anger are normal reactions for many newcomers to the South.

Whether you are newly arrived or a longtime resident, this book will help you understand the South. With understanding, we hope, will come greater appreciation for the rare and valuable qualities that are part of Southern life. Among the authors of this book are non-Southerners whose roots lie in the Midwest, the Far West, the Northeast, and even in Brooklyn. They shared others' initial impressions, but all adjusted happily to the South. They all began to consider themselves Southerners and found living in the South to be both satisfying and fascinating.

First impressions, however, are sometimes disconcerting. Differences of attitude or outlook appear in conversation, as Southerners make comments or ask questions that non-Southerners do not expect. Though trivial in themselves, such small matters point toward larger differences. They produce confusion and leave non-Southerners feeling like outsiders. Some new arrivals even conclude that "the South is like a foreign country."

For example, when they meet strangers, Southerners often show little interest in their occupations. Instead of asking, "What do you do?" they ask, "Where are you from?" Southerners ask about your religion. Although such questions would be considered impolite in some parts of the United States, Southerners will ask, "What church have you joined?" or invite you to visit their congregations. Another striking difference in religious practices is the custom of ending public prayer, even in large Southern cities, with the words, "In Jesus' name we pray. Amen." (This may happen even when Jewish people are present on the platform.)

Southerners are very polite and personable in shops and stores. Non-Southern customers who are used to rude treatment from sales clerks notice a wonderful change in the South. In stores Southerners are adept at an "aw shucks" kind of hospitality and can talk at great length about almost nothing. (Some seem reluctant to get down to business and would rather talk about the weather.)

After living in the South for several months, however, non-Southerners may begin to notice a formidable reserve. "You can't really get to know them," say some newcomers. "They don't let you into their circle." The non-Southerners who make these comments feel unwelcome and wonder if they are viewed as modern-day carpetbaggers.

The influence of history *is* tangible in the South. Some white Southerners still feel strongly about the Civil War, an event that many non-Southerners know only through books. Few Southerners ever were confused about which side won and which side lost, or where this bloodiest of America's many wars was fought. Their stance may seem excessively proud or defiant to new residents.

Southerners can be strangely defensive in other ways. They bitterly resent criticism of their communities, even if they *do* need more restaurants or better facilities. Non-Southerners who are openly critical are sometimes made to feel unwelcome in the normally hospitable South.

What do these differences mean? What do incidents like these reveal about the South? In the chapters that follow, the authors will attempt to explain the distinctive features of the South. They will do so with information and analysis, but also through personal experience and anecdotes that express the special qualities of life in the South.

Chapters 1, 2, and 3 focus on the connection between the South's special character, its history, and certain social and racial patterns that have made the Southern experience different. They treat, in order, the region's history, its sociology, and race. Chapters 4 through 7 look more closely at particular aspects of the South: the character of and attitudes toward its urban places; the nature of sex roles in the home and workplace; the changing political system; and economic development.

The authors hope that these essays will lead readers to make their own discoveries about the South, to understand it better, and to contribute more fully to its unique society. They are grateful to the many non-Southerners who helped them, as residents and professional students of the South, to learn more about this important and interesting region.

This book grew out of a series of public programs sponsored by the North Carolina Humanities Council and the South Carolina Humanities Council. We gratefully acknowledge their support and the assistance of their able staffs, particularly Brent Glass and Leland Cox. Additional financial support came from Ciba-Geigy and The Jones Group. The International Studies Program at the University of North Carolina at Charlotte provided invaluable assistance in planning and making local arrangements. We wish to thank its director, Harold Josephson, and staff members Levela Rickard, Judy Case, and Marian Beane, who were very helpful and always pleasant.

The South for New Southerners

The Special Place of History

PAUL D. ESCOTT

Southern people are much like people everywhere, but their region and its history also set them apart. The South has had a history and experience different from the rest of America, and therefore the regional culture that has evolved there is different, too.

Everyone knows about the South's warm climate, the institution of slavery, the Confederacy, and perhaps the historic importance of cotton and agriculture in the region. Other features that have affected Southern life include the persistently rural character of settlement patterns and of society in general. It has also proved significant that the great waves of immigration in the nineteenth and early twentieth centuries bypassed the South.

Many of the individual elements that make the South distinctive are not unique there. (Small towns and rural farming communities share common features throughout America.) The South is also varied; it is not everywhere the same. But a particular combination of experiences and characteristics has made the South different from all other American regions. If you keep the special features of its history in mind, you will be able to understand the region better.

A Rural Society

The South was always a rural region, and even today the impress of country life remains strong. Native Southerners are a rural people, deeply rooted in a particular locality and closely connected to family members and kin who live nearby. This accounts for much of the personalism of Southern social relations: most Southerners are not accustomed to dealing coldly or impersonally with others, even with strangers or those of differing social status.

The rural character of the South took shape with the first European settlement, as tobacco planters and their laborers in Virginia spread out along the shores and inlets of the Chesapeake to take advantage of the available water transportation for their crops. From then on, most historical and economic forces worked in favor of a dispersion rather than a concentration of people. The wealth that accrued from rice and other plantation crops encouraged farmers to operate on a large scale, and after 1793 Eli Whitney's gin made possible the cotton boom that spread the plantation economy throughout the states bordering the Gulf of Mexico.

Thus Southerners, black and white, were mostly farmers, whether as free or unfree laborers, or as owners or tenants of the farms they worked. Most white Southerners in the Slave South were not slaveowners, but even those that were tended to live on the frontier or be thoroughly accustomed to rural conditions. Many "yeoman farmers," as they were called, moved steadily on with the advance of the frontier, clearing new land and then selling it as latecomers arrived. They could not stand to be "crowded in" and hated to hear "the sound of another person's ax." Nonslaveholders who were content to stay in the older districts often lived in the vicinity of parents, siblings, and other relatives. But the desire to own one's own farm and the amount of land needed to support livestock that fed on the open range kept habitations fairly far apart. Also, for most of the nineteenth century, there was so much good land available farther west that Southerners generally kept moving on rather than accept small, worn-out farms.

We tend to forget just how rural the South was on the eve of the Civil War. Of Southern cities in 1860, only the venerable and great port of New Orleans had over 100,000 residents. Charleston numbered just 41,000, Richmond 38,000, and Mobile 29,000. Frederick Law Olmsted, who later became famous as the designer of New York City's Central Park, traveled through the South in the 1850s and saw, as he passed from Georgia into Alabama, "a hilly wilderness, with a few dreary villages, and many isolated cotton farms." Even in parts of eastern Virginia, Olmsted reported, "For hours and hours one has to ride through the unlimited, continual, all-shadowing, all-embracing forest, following roads in the making of which no more labor has been given than was necessary to remove the timber which would obstruct the passage of wagons; and even for days and days he may sometimes travel and see never two dwellings of mankind within sight of each other."

Frederick Law Olmsted's journey through the South was instructive in another way. This intelligent man was always getting lost, despite frequently asking for directions. His problem stemmed from the kind of directions Southerners gave him: they were minutely specific. They led him from a creek to some fallen trees, past an old cabin, through a gate opposite a schoolhouse, beyond a large rock, and so on. Such directions drew on the detailed knowledge of a particular locale that was second nature to residents but was beyond Olmsted's grasp. As a stranger, he could not distinguish among all the features of a foreign landscape, but the Southerners he met knew their rural neighborhoods like the backs of their hands.

Southerners typically know a great deal about all the people in their districts as well. In rural areas and small towns, many people can recall the family histories of their neighbors, black or white, and explain who married whose grandmother and how two dissimilar individuals might actually be related. This trait is noticeably apparent in Theodore Rosengarten's award-winning book, *All God's Dangers*, a fascinating oral history of a black share-cropper who was born in 1885 and lived into the 1960s. The appearance of any new character in this narrative occasions a brief, but sometimes complex, disquisition in genealogy. Such digressions baffle young urban students of either race who read the book today, but they suggest the intimate and personal knowledge that Southerners traditionally have had of their local area and its people.

The ramifications of these habits of personalism are highly significant for today's South. For example, in North Carolina's largest city, Charlotte, the chamber of commerce recently sponsored a series of workshops for owners of new and small businesses. The object was to help the owners find ways to develop customers and clients, and most of the advice concerned how to meet people and become known in the community. In response to one question, a spokesman for the chamber of commerce cut to the heart of the matter. "Southerners," he explained, "don't do business with folks they don't know." That was some consolation to an ambitious businesswoman whose extensive advertising and first-rate credentials had brought her few customers. The significance of personalism helped explain how a local competitor who did not advertise (not even with a sign on his building) had more orders than he could handle.

The personalism of social relations and the closeness of many Southern communities help to explain the ambiguous feelings non-Southerners have toward the friendly but hard-to-get-to-know natives. Such comments as "It takes a long time to be accepted" simply point to the fact that a newcomer is not yet part of the close-knit local community. He or she can be welcome but still not belong. Proving that one truly is part of the community, and not merely passing through, is often a matter of time.

A young investment counselor who located in Greenville, South Carolina, had enormous difficulty making a living for a few years. People were friendly, but they gave him no business. (After all, when are trust and familiarity more important than in selecting an investment counselor?) In time, however, this man's career turned completely around. A local client or two appeared, prospered under his guidance, and brought in large numbers of their friends, causing the young man to say, "Southerners are the most loyal, supportive people I've found." He had become a member of the community.

The Burdens of Southern History

Americans in general do not greatly value history. Rather, a tenet of our national creed has been that America is exempt from the restrictions and limitations imposed by history. Unlike the Old World, America represented a fresh start, unlimited opportunity, the creation of a new and better society. The spirit of renewal and boundless optimism of Americans have been widely noted.

This has not been so for the South. As C. Vann Woodward, the dean of Southern historians, has pointed out, the South experienced history in the Old World sense of suffering, blasted hopes, and defeat rather than rising expectations. Southerners lived for a long time with pervasive, continuing poverty. History unfolded for them in distinctly unpleasant and long-lasting ways.

The Civil War brought black Southerners their freedom, an invaluable prize, but for many white Southerners it was a signal disaster. In a conflict that cost more American lives than World War II and virtually all other U.S. wars combined, the Confederacy lost almost as many men as the Union, though it had little more than one-half the population. Much property was destroyed or lost—and not just that belonging to slaveholders. Nonslaveholding small farmers lost a large portion of their holdings through the destruction of livestock.

Even more significant for white attitudes was the lasting stigma that attached to the Confederacy as the loser in America's greatest war. Victory confers a seal of approval on the winning side, and many Northerners had taken into the Civil War the sincere conviction that their section of the country was vibrant and progressive, whereas the South had a backward and undemocratic social system. Thus the outcome of the conflict burdened the white South with an unflattering image for generations to come.

If you encounter a white Southerner who is passionate about the Civil War, or who refers to it half in jest as "the Warrh," "the War between the States," or "the War of Northern Aggression," do not be surprised. Remember that the nation made the white South pay throughout subsequent generations for its errors in seceding from the Union and then losing the war. Recall that Lyndon Johnson, like scores of other Southern politicians, knew that he had no chance of being elected president until tragedy elevated him to that office. His accent was wrong, his intelligence subject to question, his attitudes probably deplorable. The rest of the nation looked down on Southerners as inferior and blameworthy, and Southerners knew it. Jimmy Carter's election may have proved that one barrier had fallen, but his Southern background was not always an asset.

Many of the unflattering stereotypes of the South grew out of the decades of poverty and economic stagnation that followed the Civil War. Southerners often tended to blame their region's poverty on the war itself, saying that it had set them back and cost them ground they were still trying to recover. We know now that other factors, including the cost of maintaining white supremacy and segregation, played a much greater role.

The unevenly distributed but booming prosperity of the antebellum South had rested on the voracious appetite of English textile mills for Southern cotton. Britain was then the most industrialized country in the world, and the textile industry was its leading sector. Each year the demand for cotton rose so much that Southerners never could grow enough, and the fortunes of planters steadily accumulated even as the number of growers kept increasing.

At approximately the time of the Civil War, however, the English textile industry penetrated the last of the major world markets for textile products. Thereafter, during the post–Civil War period in this country, the demand for cotton increased at a much slower rate. After the war, Southerners struggled against competition from Egyptian and Indian planters but managed to regain their dominant position in the world's production of cotton. They even began to produce far more cotton than ever before. But their triumph of productivity now brought only declining prices as supply exceeded demand.

Worse still, Southern agriculturalists were locked into growing cotton by the crop-lien system. Under this arrangement, a "furnishing merchant" advanced farmers the food and supplies they needed while their crops were growing but retained first claim on the crops at harvest. To be assured of recovering his loans, the merchant customarily demanded that the farmers grow cotton, the predictable money crop. Southern agriculture entered a long depression, and because most Southerners were farmers, the region's economy as a whole remained depressed. In 1938 President Franklin D. Roosevelt declared that the South was the nation's "Number One" economic problem, and the transformation of the Southern economy did not get underway until after World War II.

What about the "New South"—the South of industry and textile mills that Atlanta newspaper editor Henry Grady and others had been trumpeting since the 1870s and 1880s? This New South was real; beginning in the late nineteenth century, industry grew as rapidly in the South as it did in the rest of the nation. But its impact was limited for three reasons. First, Southern industry built upon a very small base, so although growth was rapid, cumulative size remained small for many years. Second, black workers were barred from the textile industry altogether and were granted few opportunities to participate in other developing industries. Third, the rate of natural increase of the South's population was very high. In fact, through most of this century the South exported large numbers of people to other parts of the nation yet still continued to grow. Thus New South industry was not able to transform a growing population still largely dependent on agriculture.

How have these economic forces shaped today's region? For one thing, because poverty fostered many negative stereotypes, Southerners are naturally sensitive to criticism about the quality of their institutions and services. Before you criticize, remember that Southerners have had a long struggle up from poverty and still have a long way to go. Many Southern states rank near the bottom in national listings of money spent on education and other public services; if states were ranked by the size of their tax bases, Southern states would be near the bottom of that list too.

Some Southerners like John Shelton Reed, the author of chapter 2 in this book, manage to carry the burden of the region's economic history lightly. Reed belongs to the Society for the Preservation of the Hookworm, a group dedicated to protecting a threatened Southern creature from the onslaught of Yankee progress. But in fact, Southern poverty has been a real burden. Mississippi, one of the poorest states in the nation, inaugurated a statewide kindergarten program only in 1983. No doubt racism helped delay this step, but it is also true that, compared with other states, Mississippi could not easily afford such a program earlier.

A new resident of North Carolina, recently arrived from California, remarked on the puny appearance of the two-lane state roads and highways. These state highways may not compare favorably with western freeways, but they nevertheless represent more miles of paved road than any other Southern state can boast. A relatively poor Southern state, North Carolina made a very large effort to provide for its citizens and earned the title of the Good Roads State. Given circumstances like these, it is easier to understand why Southerners may not take kindly to judgments that their facilities are too small, inadequate, or inferior to those of other places.

The historically weak economy of the South may also be responsible for some of the region's more desirable, humane traits. Southerners tend to take more time with people—even busy and highly productive Southerners appear to enjoy conversation and know how to be gracious. Many Southerners also know how to sit back and observe the spectacle of life instead of constantly pushing toward a self-imposed goal. They know how to watch and learn as well as to do, and that may be an important form of wisdom.

These abilities may have developed from the circumstances of life in a stagnant economy; at least they made such a life more rewarding. In William Faulkner's novel *The Hamlet*, much of the "action" consists of men sitting and slowly talking on the porch of the village's only store. In Faulkner's South, nothing much was going on (and much of the change that did occur was bad, as individuals steadily fell into debt and lost their farms). As a consequence, people learned to observe the human drama, to watch the actions and interactions of other people. They were perceptive amateur sociologists, if you will. They also learned to enjoy a good story and to take pleasure in the art of conversation, an art too often lost in today's busy world.

The Effects of Racial and Social Inequality

Americans are aware that Southern history and Southern life have been deeply marked by racial injustice. After all, the South was the land of slavery and then of segregation, and generations of non-Southerners have liked to think that racial oppression was a peculiar, un-American phenomenon confined to the South. Though mistaken about the regional limitations of racism, these non-Southerners certainly are correct that racial inequities have pervaded Southern history.

The effects of racism have been long-lasting and are very much with the South today. Non-Southerners will notice many signs of progress in Southern race relations: by several measures, the South today is clearly ahead of the rest of the nation rather than behind it. But there is a large legacy of injustice yet to overcome, and careful observers will soon notice the problems that remain as well as the progress that is familiar. Racism is still a part of life in the South, as it is in the rest of the nation, and its legacy will be visible for decades to come.

Another important, though often overlooked, fact about Southern history is that there has been pronounced inequality and conflict between whites in the South as well. Southern leaders always insisted that the opposite was true. The need to unite all whites, first against threats of slave insurrection and later in the name of white supremacy, produced repeated assertions that all whites were equal in status, brothers by virtue of their race. John C. Calhoun was one of the earliest in a long line of Southern leaders to make these claims.

Yet wealth has been very unequally distributed among whites throughout most of Southern history. Opportunities were only selectively available from the Civil War until recent decades. Not surprisingly, there has been conflict, the most visible manifestation being the Populist movement. Faulkner's *The Hamlet* describes the basic conditions that produced Populism. Of Will Varner, the wealthiest man in a poverty-stricken county that could have been almost any Southern county for decades around the 1890s, Faulkner writes:

[He] was the chief man of the country. He was the largest landholder and beat supervisor in one county and Justice of the Peace in the next and election commissioner in both, and hence the fountainhead if not of law at least of advice and suggestion. . . . He was a farmer, a usurer, a veterinarian; Judge Benbow of Jefferson once said of him that a milder-mannered man never bled a mule or stuffed a ballot box. He owned most of the good land in the country and held mortgages on most of the rest. He owned the store and the cotton gin and the grist mill and blacksmith shop in the village proper and it was considered, to put it mildly, bad luck for a man to do his trading or gin his cotton or grind his meal or shoe his stock anywhere else.

The Will Varners prospered in an era when most lost ground.

As thousands of yeoman farmers fell into debt, lost their farms, and became tenants, they began to join the Farmers' Alliance and demand basic changes affecting money and credit. When the Democratic party failed to embrace Alliance proposals, angry white farmers organized a Populist party that cooperated with black Republicans and shook Southern politics to its foundations. But at the end of the 1890s, the Populists were beaten by the mainline Democrats. In many cases they were suppressed with such force and such blatant fraud that, by 1920, the largest concentration of socialists in America was to be found among still-resentful former Populists in Oklahoma, Arkansas, and Texas.

Thus, both blacks and whites had the experience of growing up in a society whose fundamental arrangements were a source of deep grievance to many people. These grievances also were matters that many felt they could not change. Slaves resented their oppression and several times rose in rebellion, but most individual slaves and most poor whites lived and died with the consciousness that elite power was too formidable to overcome. After disfranchisement and the defeat of Populism, blacks and dissident white Southerners also knew that their cause was practically hopeless. The region's troubled economy provided little or no opportunity for generations of Southerners.

Resentments are never far beneath the surface of such a society as this. As one Southern historian (who is also a Southerner) has noted, Southerners knew that they were living on top of a powder keg, and they had to find ways to manage the tension. Two common solutions were to muffle conflict through courtesy and apparent cordiality and to avoid conflict entirely through indirection and tact.

It is no accident that Southerners have been renowned for their courtesy. Nor should it seem strange that the Southern poor, especially, were recognized as consummate practitioners of the art of good manners. They had to be. To survive, the poor and weak of both races often had to mollify hostile or threatening elites. Their prospects in life depended directly upon their adept and tactful dealing with persons who had power over them. Consider the realities of power in a county like the one described by Faulkner. Could an ordinary person oppose or stand up to a Will Varner? Not if he or she wanted to avoid trouble!

Non-Southerners eventually learn that in the South people tend to communicate by indirection. Southerners are raised to be polite and respectful of authority. They try to avoid saying no, and they prefer seeming agreement to open conflict or rejection. Southerners' silences often speak louder than their words. Their actions may reveal less enthusiasm than their agreeable manners suggest.

In many parts of the United States, it is perfectly acceptable in business discussions to say, "I disagree with that completely," or "That won't work; I think we should take the opposite approach." Such frank conversations do not occur in the ordinary Southern workplace. Many transplanted Northerners have found themselves mired in a long meeting to consider a simply dreadful or unworkable proposal. To their surprise, the terrible idea is treated politely, even respectfully; people seem positive about it. But after the meeting no one lifts a finger to pursue the proposal. Communication took place, but by indirection and with a politeness that can be baffling to some new arrivals.

The differences in communication styles may cause some non-Southerners to have difficulty establishing comfortable relationships with their coworkers. The newcomer's normal candor may strike Southerners as aggressive or pushy behavior. Comments from a Southern coworker that are intended as helpful suggestions may go unnoticed. Jokes and repartee may not be immediately comprehensible. The best course for the non-Southerner is to be patient and observe the ways in which Southerners deal with each other. Watching attentively will probably yield more information than direct confrontation over an issue.

Before non-Southerners become familiar with the indirection that characterizes Southern social relations, they sometimes draw erroneous conclusions from their daily experiences. One new resident who needed some work done on his house contacted a highly recommended contractor. Although homeowners everywhere can have difficulty tying laborers down to a definite appointment, this case was particularly trying. The contractor agreed to come on certain days but never did. In exasperation the homeowner concluded that Southerners do not know how to run a business: They are "slipshod" and "unreliable," he said. Perhaps the contractor was, but more likely he was simply reluctant to give a disappointing and possibly inaccurate answer.

The place of small talk in business conversations is another area of difference. To Southerners, small talk is an essential lubricant of the social system. It is never dispensed with in order to get down to more important matters. "Getting to the point" with Southerners may delay that goal considerably. The careful listener may also discern that apparently aimless pleasantries sometimes constitute the heart of a conversation, as Southerners feel each other out and indirectly discover what they need to know.

Maddening though these patterns of communication may be for the uninitiated, they are understandable developments in a society that evolved around major racial and social inequalities. Courtesy, tact, and indirection helped a deeply divided society to function, and they still ease social intercourse today.

Many Evangelicals, Few Ethnics

The religious and ethnic composition of the South began to diverge markedly from that of the rest of the nation before the Civil War, and the effects are still very evident today. After industrialization took hold in the Northern economy, thousands of jobs were created in large industrial cities. Immigrants—many of whom were Catholic or Jewish—came penniless to those cities to get a start in America. The South's economy was foundering in the 1870s and 1880s, when millions of Italians, Poles, Russians, and others were crossing the ocean. Because the Southern economy remained troubled until after the passage of restrictive immigration laws in 1924, the steadily increasing supply of ethnic Americans continued to bypass the South.

As a result, most Southerners have not historically been Irish, Italian, German, Polish, or Russian in origin, and there are very few Catholics or Jews in the region. Southerners, black and white, are overwhelmingly Protes-

" THAT'S RIGHT— JIM AND TAMMY WERE EXPELLED FROM PARADISE AND LEFT ME IN CHARGE ! "

tant, and among these, Baptists and Methodists predominate by such a large margin that the tag "Bible Belt" is long established. Not all Southerners are fundamentalists, but most are evangelical Protestants who are used to living among others of similar persuasion.

A few years ago, a history class in North Carolina was discussing the religious beliefs of the Puritans who founded Massachusetts. As the discussion turned to the Puritans' hostility to Catholic theology, one young woman became noticeably perplexed. After trying to sort out her confusion, she raised her hand and asked, with total sincerity, "Are Catholics Christians?" A reminder that Protestants protested the beliefs and practices of the Catholic church brought her back to facts she had once known. But her confusion was genuine and understandable. This student simply had little or no actual acquaintance with Catholics. She had grown up in a small town in North Carolina, which received the smallest number of nineteenth-century immigrants in the entire South. Probably all the people she knew as she grew up were Baptists, Methodists, or members of some other Protestant denomination. Like all of us, she remembered best the information that she used regularly, rather than the unused facts stored away in her memory.

Lack of experience with non-Protestants accounts for many Southern comments on religion. It is normal practice in many communities to praise good, caring, or compassionate people as "Christian people," because Christian ideals are the dominant models for conduct. If asked, many Southerners would agree that Jewish, Hindu, or Buddhist individuals can be good people, too, but such people are not very visible in nonmetropolitan parts of the South. Likewise, the assumption—careless but historically understandable—that all in attendance at a gathering are Christians explains references to Jesus in public prayers.

When Southerners ask strangers what church they attend, their intention is not to pry but to be friendly. The South has not experienced persistent Protestant/Catholic conflict in the way the Northeast has, so it is not forbidden to ask about church. In addition, church attendance in the South is higher than the national norm. These numbers may indicate that Southerners are more devout than other Americans, but they probably also stem from the rural and small-town nature of the South. In many Southern communities, church is a major center of social activity as well as worship. Socializing, courtship, and recreation are connected with church activities, and thus inviting a stranger to church is also an invitation to be part of the community as well.

Although these are reassuring thoughts, it also must be noted that the narrow range of Southerners' religious experiences can produce some limited perspectives. All people grow through challenge or exposure to change, and Southerners whose experience has been restricted cannot be expected to achieve a cosmopolitan perspective immediately. Pat Robertson supports religious freedom for all, but one wonders whether the school prayer that he advocates could as well be a Jewish or Hindu or Islamic prayer as a Christian one. Robertson and many of his supporters may not have thought through all the ramifications of publicly endorsed school prayer in a diverse society.

It is also apparent that the enormous changes sweeping over the South today will alarm some devout Southerners and create possibilities for cultural conflict. Change is always unsettling to human societies, and the extremes of change in today's United States are found in the South. Fears about improper teachings in the public schools—sex education, evolution, or "secular humanism"—have surfaced both in diverse urban areas and in sleepy communities that are now being exposed to rapid change. Increased contacts between Southerners and non-Southerners may, at least in the short run, augment perceptions of difference. Some conflict may be inevitable.

Non-Southerners and the South's Future

The above reflections lead naturally to the question of what role non-Southerners will play in the unprecedented transformation that is taking place in the South. The changes now remaking the South's economy are as great in scale as any that have ever affected an American region, and correspondingly the impact on habits, values, and ways of life are profound. New Southerners, in one sense a symptom of the transformation, are also residents who have much at stake.

Southerners are delighted with many of the changes underway. Naturally they are glad to leave behind the poverty and stagnant economy that plagued the region for generations. Though many white Southerners fought to hold onto segregation, the lifting of the cloud of Jim Crow has had innumerable good effects. Few Southerners (least of all the leaders of the business community) want to turn the clock back. Change has given Southerners more of the good things in life and, in addition, a new image and new self-confidence.

But the modern transformation of the South inevitably is affecting ways of thought and life that endured for generations. If poverty and racism can be gladly dispensed with, what about the sense of rootedness and the strong ties to family, kin, and community that accompanied a rural culture and substantial social homogeneity? A region that was, by census definitions, two-thirds rural in 1940 had become two-thirds urban by 1970. Farming, the largest sector of employment as late as 1957, now accounts for only 5 percent or less of Southern workers. With dramatic economic growth have come hundreds of thousands of in-migrants from other regions of the United States and various parts of the world who have brought their own cultural backgrounds and helped to diversify the religious and ethnic homogeneity that facilitated close-knit social relations.

Many Southern families are confronting painful choices between things

"WELL, NOW, THAT'S RIGHT GENEROUS OF YOU, BROTHER JESSE, BUT WHAT IF SOUTH CAROLINA DON'T WANNA BE SET FREE?!"

they value. A young couple who live next to the wife's parents on rural land in their home county must decide whether to accept a promotion and transfer to Atlanta for the benefit of one of their careers. They cannot have both increased prosperity and the close ties to place and community that they have established. As more elements in the economy become national or global in scope, more Southerners will have to face these dilemmas.

Through will and force of circumstance, Southerners forged many of their most valuable traits out of regional disadvantages. Through hardship many individuals developed endurance and patience. Southern literature is full of fiercely independent characters who live in dependent circumstances, and this literature accurately reflects Southern life. Many Southerners have done the best they could, knowing full well that the results would not be all they desired. But from poverty and lack of opportunity, they learned better to appreciate family and friends, nature, and the human rather than the material riches of life.

The world needs these Southern values, especially the sense of place or rootedness that is vital to Southern culture. A glance at any day's newspaper shows all too clearly that many people in the modern world feel cut off from all communities. They feel isolated and alienated, and, lacking a sense of belonging, they act in socially or personally destructive ways. The South's sense of place and the warmth and personalism of its human relations are qualities that need to be preserved and cultivated.

The choice ultimately rests with the people who live in the South. They can choose which values to keep and which to replace. They can, if they are sensitive to the challenge, retain the best of the traditional South while accepting desirable elements of change. In this process, newly arrived Southerners will have a large effect on the outcome.

The fact that you are reading this book is a positive sign. It shows that you are curious and ready to learn, and therefore the chances are that you can adapt happily and successfully to a distinctive American region. As you learn about the South, take seriously the heritage that it has to offer. As you live in the South, give thought to how you can help this region fuse the best of its past with the opportunities of the future.

The South
What Is It? *Where* Is It?

J O H N   S H E L T O N   R E E D

So you've moved, or been moved, to the South. Or maybe you're thinking about it. You're wondering: What is this place? What's different about it? *Is* it different, anymore? Good questions—old ones, too. People have been asking them for decades. Some of us even make our livings by asking them, but we still don't agree about the answers. Let's look at what might seem to be a simpler question: Where is the South?

That's easy enough, isn't it? People more or less agree about which parts of the United States are in the South and which aren't. If I gave you a list of states and asked which ones are "Southern," all in all, chances are you'd agree with some of my students, whose answers are summarized in figure 1. I don't share their hesitation about Kentucky and Arkansas, and I think too many were ready to put Missouri in the South, but there's not a lot to argue with here.

That tells us something. It tells us that the South is, to begin with, a concept—and a shared one. It's an idea that people can talk about, think about, use to orient themselves and each other. People know whether they're in it or not. As a geographer would put it, the South is a "vernacular" region.

Let's stop and think about that. Why should that be so? Why can I write "South" with some assurance that people will know I mean Richmond and don't mean Phoenix? What is it that the South's boundaries enclose?

FIGURE I. *Percentage Who Say Each State Is Southern, "All in All"*

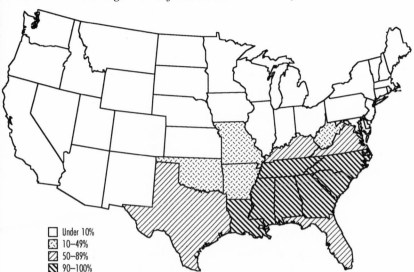

Under 10%
10–49%
50–89%
90–100%

Source: 68 students at the University of North Carolina at Chapel Hill

Well, for starters, it's not news that the South has been an economically and demographically distinctive place—a poor, rural region with a biracial population, reflecting the historic dominance of the plantation system. One thing the South's boundaries have set off is a batch of distinctive problems growing out of that history. Those problems are becoming less and less obvious, but most are still with us to some extent, and we can still use them to locate the South.

But the South is more than just a collection of unfavorable statistics. It has also been home to several populations, black and white, whose intertwined cultures have set them off from other Americans as well as from each other. Some of us, in fact, have suggested that Southerners ought to be viewed as an American ethnic group, like Italian or Polish Americans. If we can use distinctive cultural attributes to find Southerners, then we can say that the South is where they are found. Southerners are also like members of immigrant ethnic groups in that they have a sense of group identity based on their shared history and their cultural distinctiveness in the present. If we could locate it, one of the best boundaries for the South would be what Hamilton Horton calls the "Hell, yes!" line—where people begin to answer that way when asked if they're Southerners.

Finally, to the considerable extent that people do have a sense of the South's existence, its distinctiveness, and its boundaries, various regional institutions have contributed heavily. Southern businesses, Southern magazines, Southern voluntary associations, Southern colleges and universities—many of these have aspired to serve the South as a whole. We can map the South by looking at where their influence extends.

These are all plausible ways to go about answering the question, Where is the South? For the most part, they give similar answers, which is reassuring. But it's where they differ (as they sometimes do) that they're most likely to tell us something about what the South has been and is becoming. Nobody would exclude Mississippi from the South. But is Texas now a Southern state? Is Florida, anymore? How about West Virginia?

Allow me a homely simile. The South is like my favorite pair of blue jeans. It has shrunk some, faded a bit, gotten a few holes in it. There's always the possibility that it might split at the seams. It doesn't look much like it used to, but it's more comfortable now, and there's probably a lot of wear left in it.

The Socioeconomic South

"Let us begin by discussing the weather," wrote U. B. Phillips in 1929. The weather, that distinguished Southern historian asserted,

> has been the chief agency in making the South distinctive. It fostered the cultivation of the staple crops, which promoted the plantation system, which brought the importation of Negroes, which not only gave rise to chattel slavery but created a lasting race problem. These led to controversy and regional rivalry for power, which . . . culminated in a stroke for independence.

FIGURE 2. *Where Kudzu Grows*

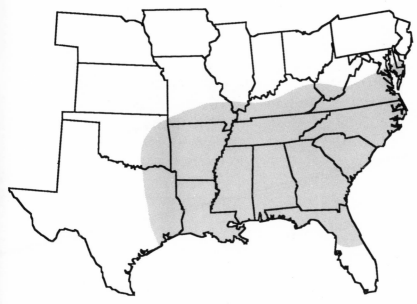

Source: John J. Winberry and David M. Jones, "Rise and Decline of the 'Miracle Vine': Kudzu in the Southern Landscape," *Southeastern Geographer* 13 (Nov. 1973): 62.

Phillips and the many who have shared his views see almost everything of interest about the South as emanating from this complex of plantation, black population, Civil War—thus, ultimately, from the weather.

Obviously, it's hot here in the summer, and humid. Some vegetable life loves that. Kudzu, for instance—that rampant, loopy vine needs long, moist summers, and it gets them in the South. "Where kudzu grows" (fig. 2) isn't a bad definition of the South (and notice that it doesn't grow in Florida or West Texas). But another plant has been far more consequential for the South. That plant, of course, is cotton. Dixie *was* "the land of cotton," and figure 3 shows that in the early years of this century Southerners grew cotton nearly everywhere they could grow it: in any place that had two hundred or more frost-free days a year, annual precipitation of twenty-three inches or more, and soil that wasn't sand. Certainly, cotton culture affected the racial makeup of the South and slowed the growth of Southern cities. Figure 4 shows what the region looked like, demographically, in 1920. Few cities interrupted the

FIGURE 3. *Acres of Cotton Cultivation, 1909*

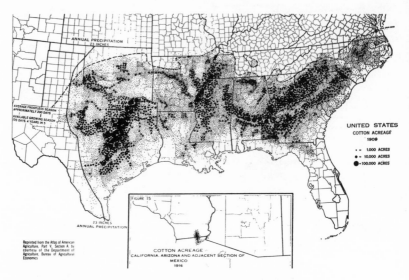

Source: U.S. Department of Agriculture, Bureau of Agricultural Economics
Note: Map also shows gradients for precipitation and frost-free days.

FIGURE 4. *The Demography of the South, 1920*

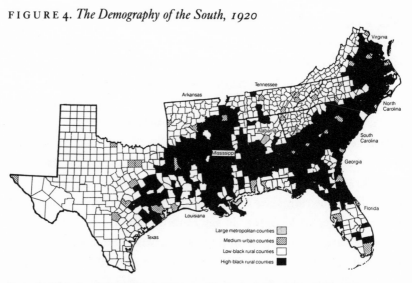

Source: Earl Black and Merle Black, *Politics and Society in the South* (Cambridge, Mass..
Harvard University Press, 1987), 36.

FIGURE 5. *Lynchings, 1900–1930*

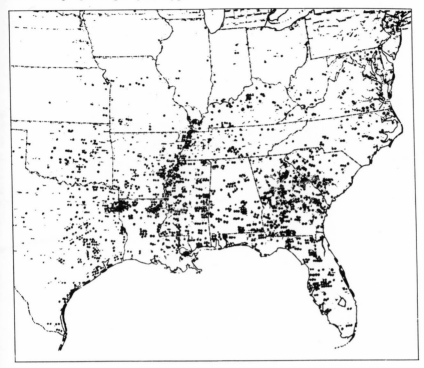

Source: Southern Commission on the Study of Lynching

countryside. A band of rural counties with substantial black populations (shaded on the map) traced the area of cotton cultivation and plantation agriculture in a long arc, from southeastern Virginia down and across to eastern Texas, with arms extending north and south along the Mississippi.

This is the *Deep* South—what a geographer would call the "core area" of the region, defined by its staple-crop economy. Here some Southern characteristics and phenomena were found in their purest, most concentrated forms. Lynchings, for example (fig. 5). Or peculiar, single-issue politics (that issue, as a politician once put it, "spelled n-i-g-g-e-r"), reflected in support for the futile candidacies of third-party or unpopular major-party presidential candidates (fig. 6). For decades the Deep South shaped Southern culture and politics and, still more, shaped people's image of what the South was all about.

FIGURE 6. *Unusual Voting in Presidential Elections, 1928–1968*

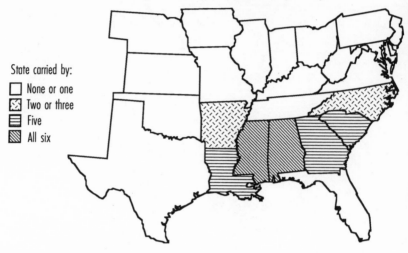

State carried by:
- ☐ None or one
- ☒ Two or three
- ▤ Five
- ▨ All six

Note: Unusual voting is defined as a vote for one of the following candidates: Al Smith (Democrat, 1928); Strom Thurmond (States' Rights, 1948); Adlai Stevenson (Democrat, 1952); Adlai Stevenson (Democrat, 1956); Barry Goldwater (Republican, 1964); George Wallace (American Independent, 1968).

FIGURE 7. *The Demography of the South, 1980*

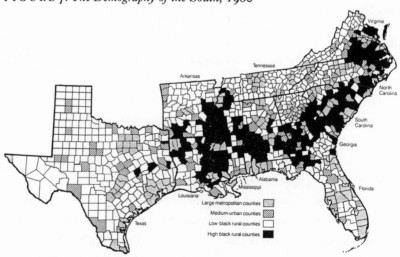

Large metropolitan counties
Medium-urban counties
Low-black rural counties
High-black rural counties

Source: Earl Black and Merle Black, *Politics and Society in the South* (Cambridge, Mass.: Harvard University Press, 1987), 38.

FIGURE 8. *Housing Units without Complete Plumbing, 1980*

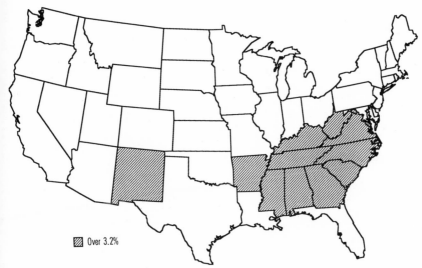

☒ Over 3.2%

Source: Data from *Statistical Abstract of the United States, 1982–83*, 755.
Note: A unit without complete plumbing is defined as having no flush toilet, no bathtub or shower, or no hot and cold running water.

Two out of three Southerners today are urban folk, and most rural Southerners work in industry anyway, but the fossil remains of this old South can still be found as concentrations of poor, rural black Southerners (compare fig. 7 to fig. 4). These pockets, together with concentrations of poor, rural *white* Southerners in the Southern highlands, ensure that most Southern states are still at the bottom of the U.S. per-capita income distribution. (Virginia, Texas, and Florida—all barely involved in plantation agriculture and with little or no mountain population—are exceptions.) This means, in turn, that almost any problem of poor people, or of poor states, can still be used to map the South. Everything from outdoor toilets (fig. 8) to illiteracy (fig. 9) to bad teeth (fig. 10) costs money to put right, and many Southern people and most Southern states still don't have much.

Poverty is bad news, in general, and I certainly don't suggest that we get nostalgic about it, but it has had one or two redeeming points. Burglary rates, for example, are strikingly correlated with states' average incomes—presumably not because rich people steal but because they have more *to* steal—and

FIGURE 9. *Illiteracy Rates, 1970*

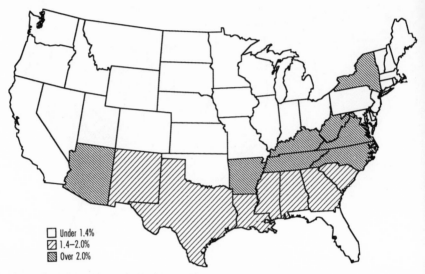

Under 1.4%
1.4–2.0%
Over 2.0%

Source: Data from *Statistical Abstract of the United States, 1981*, 143.

figure 11 shows that burglary has been relatively uncommon in all but the richest Southern states. (A policeman once offered me another explanation. Going in other people's windows is a dangerous occupation in the South, he argued. "You're likely to meet something lead coming out.")

In any case, the shadow of the plantation is now giving way to the light of the Sunbelt. The South may still be on the bottom of the socioeconomic heap, but the distance between top and bottom is smaller than it used to be. (In a few respects, South and non-South have traded places: the Southern birthrate, for instance, historically higher, is now lower than the national average.) Consequently, those who view the South primarily in economic terms are likely to believe that the region is disappearing. "Southern characteristics" that simply revealed that the South was a poor, rural region are more and more confined to pockets of poverty within the region—or, more accurately, the statistics increasingly reflect the presence of air-conditioned pockets of affluence, particularly in Texas, Florida, and a few metropolitan areas elsewhere. If we map the South with the same criteria people used even fifty years ago, what we get these days looks more like a Swiss cheese than a coherent region.

FIGURE 10. *Active Dentists per 1,000 Residents, 1982*

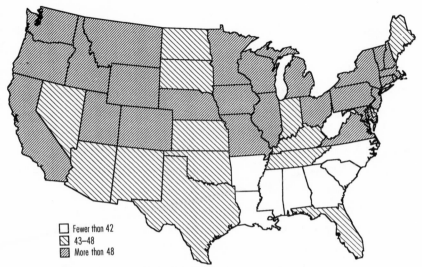

☐ Fewer than 42
◩ 43–48
▨ More than 48

Source: Data from *Statistical Abstract of the United States, 1986*, 104.

FIGURE 11. *High Burglary Rates, 1984*

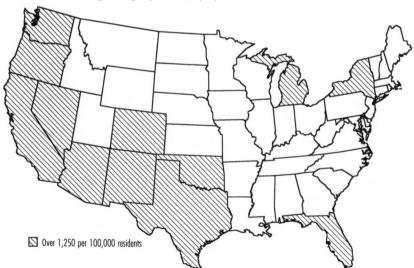

◩ Over 1,250 per 100,000 residents

Source: Data from *Statistical Abstract of the United States, 1986*, 167.

The Cultural South

But suppose we don't define the South in economic and demographic terms. What if we somehow identify Southerners and then define the South as where they come from? We could say, for example, that people who eat grits, listen to country music, follow stock-car racing, support corporal punishment in the schools, hunt 'possum, go to Baptist churches, and prefer bourbon to scotch (if they drink at all) are likely to be Southerners. It isn't necessary that all or even most Southerners do these things, or that other people not do them; if Southerners just do them more often than other Americans, we can use them to locate the South.

Look at the geographical distribution of Baptists, for example (fig. 12). Early on, members of that faith established their dominance in the Southern backcountry, in numbers approached only by those of Methodists. As Southerners moved on farther to the west and south, they took their religion with them. The map shows that there are a good many Baptists in New York, to be sure, but New York has lots of everything. Not many people live in West Texas, but those who do are likely to be Baptists. In this respect, the mountain South, too, is virtually indistinguishable from the rest of the region.

And when it comes to Southern music, the mountains and the Southwest are right at the heart of things. Figure 13 shows where country music makers come from: a fertile crescent extending from southwest Virginia through Kentucky and Tennessee to Arkansas, Oklahoma, and Texas. Musically, what is sometimes called the "peripheral" South is in fact the region's core. The *Deep* South is peripheral to the country music scene, although it's not a vacuum like New England; a similar map for traditional *black* musicians would almost certainly fill some of the gap. Country musicians' origins are reflected in the songs they produce, too. In figure 14, the size of each state is proportional to the number of times it's mentioned in country music lyrics. Notice Florida's position as a sort of appendix to the South.

Those lyrics also suggest a regional propensity for particular sorts of violence, and FBI statistics show that this isn't just talk. For as long as reliable records have been kept, the South has had a higher homicide rate than the rest of the nation, and the mountains and Southwest share fully in this

FIGURE 12. *Members of Baptist Churches, 1952*

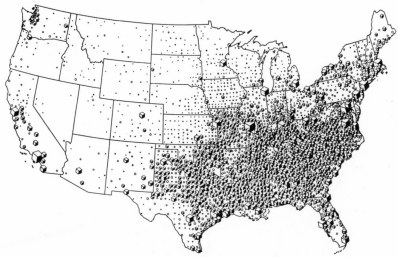

Source: Wilbur Zelinsky, "An Approach to the Religious Geography of the United States: Patterns of Church Membership in 1952," *Annals of the Association of American Geographers* 51 (June 1961): 172.

FIGURE 13. *Birthplaces of Country Music Notables, 1870–1960*

Source: George O. Carey, "T for Texas, T for Tennessee: The Origins of American Country Music Notables," *Journal of Geography* 78 (Nov. 1979): 221.

FIGURE 14. *States Mentioned in Country Music Lyrics*

Source: Ben Marsh, "A Rose-Colored Map," *Harper's*, July 1977, 80. Used by permission.
Note: The size of each state is proportional to the number of times it is mentioned.

pattern. Southern violence, however, isn't directed inward. Around the world, societies with high homicide rates tend to have low suicide rates, and the same is true for American states. It very much looks as if there is some sort of trade-off at work. Figure 15 shows that homicide is about as common as suicide is uncommon throughout the region—one of the few things the South has in common with New York.

Regional cultural differences are also reflected in family and sex-role attitudes. These differences have even surfaced in the legal system: Southern states were slow to enact women's suffrage; most never did ratify the Equal Rights Amendment; and until recently few had state laws against sex discrimination (fig. 16). Southern women have actually been more likely than other American women to work outside the home (they've needed the money more), but most often they've worked in "women's jobs"—as textile opera-

FIGURE 15. *Ratio of Homicides to Suicides, 1983*

＊ ＊   less than .25
  ＊   .25–.40
blank   .41–.55
  1   .56–.95
  2   greater than .95

Source: Data from *Statistical Abstract of the United States, 1987*, 77.

tives or domestic servants, for example. The percentage of women in predominantly male occupations remains lower in the South than elsewhere (fig. 17).

Notice that these characteristics aren't related in any obvious way to the plantation complex. Aspects of culture like diet, religion, sports, music, and family patterns don't simply reflect how people make their livings, or how good a living they make. To a great extent, they're passed on from generation to generation within families. Usually, when families move, they carry these patterns with them. That's why many Southern values and tastes and habits are found in the Appalachians, the Ozarks, and most of Texas and Oklahoma. Those areas were marginal, at best, to the plantation South, but they were settled by Southerners. Mapping cultural traits makes it easy to figure out who settled most of Missouri, too, as well as the southern parts of Illinois, Indiana, and Ohio. And many of the same features can be found in scattered enclaves of Southern migrants all around the United States—among auto workers in Ypsilanti, for instance, or the children and grandchildren of Okies in Bakersfield.

FIGURE 16. *No State Law against Sex Discrimination, 1972*

We can't expect the demise of the plantation to make these characteristics go away. So if we define the South as a patch of territory somehow different from the rest of the United States because it is inhabited by people who are different from other Americans, we still have a great deal to work with. Indeed, we have new things to work with all the time. We need to recall that country music came of age only with the phonograph and NASCAR racing only with the high-performance stock car. Consider also figure 18, which shows the distribution of colleges and universities that publish their own sports magazines. Southern institutions of higher learning have seldom been on the cutting edge of innovation, but they seem to be out front on this one.

Southern Identification

I suggested earlier that we can look at the South, not as just a distinctive economic or cultural area, but as the home of people somehow bound together by ties of loyalty and identification. Clearly, the South has been a

FIGURE 17. *Low Percentage of White Women Employed in Traditionally White Male Occupations, 1985*

Source: Data from Southern Labor Institute
Note: Shading represents the bottom ten states.

FIGURE 18. *Colleges and Universities That Publish Sports Magazines, 1982*

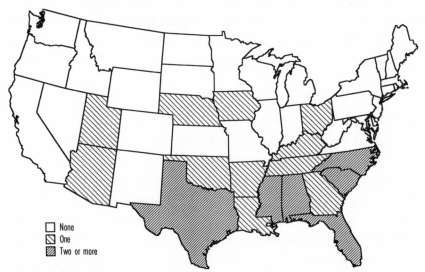

☐ None
◨ One
▨ Two or more

Source: Data from *Chronicle of Higher Education*, 15 Sept. 1982, 17.

"province" in Josiah Royce's sense of that word: "part of a national domain which is, geographically and socially, sufficiently unified to have a true consciousness of its own unity, to feel a pride in its own ideals and customs, and to possess a sense of its distinction from other parts of the country." Not long ago, the regional patriotism of most white Southerners was based on the shared experience of Confederate independence and defeat. There are still reminders of this past in the South's culture and social life. Figure 19, for example, shows where to find chapters of the Kappa Alpha Order, a college fraternity with an explicitly Confederate heritage.

For many, the word "Dixie" evokes that same heritage, and figure 20 shows where people are likely to include that word in the names of their business enterprises. Notice that the Appalachian South, which wasn't wild about Dixie in 1861, still isn't. Now the Southwest, too, has largely abandoned Dixie (turn about—the Confederacy largely abandoned the Southwest, once). Most of Florida would probably be gone as well if there were no Dixie Highway to keep the word in use. Even in the city of Atlanta, Dixie seems to be gone with the wind—or at least it's on the way out. Only in what is left of the old plantation South is Dixie really alive and well.

As a basis for identification, obviously, symbols of the Confederate experience necessarily exclude nearly all black Southerners, as well as many Appalachian whites and migrants to the region who have moved so recently that they haven't forgotten they're newcomers. Fortunately, regional loyalty can be based on other things, among them cultural differences like those we've already examined.

We can ask, in other words, not, Where do people display Southern ways? but, Where do people assert the superiority of Southern ways? Figure 21, for example, shows where people are likely to say that they like to hear Southern accents, prefer Southern food, and believe that Southern women are better looking than other women. (The Gallup Poll hasn't asked these questions lately, so the data are a little old, but I doubt that the patterns would be much different now.) The South, defined in this way, naturally coincides pretty well with the areas in which one is actually apt to encounter Southern accents, Southern food, and Southern women—a bigger region than what remains of

FIGURE 19. *Chapters of the Kappa Alpha Order, 1988*

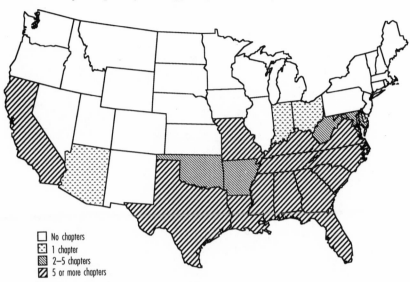

☐ No chapters
⊡ 1 chapter
▧ 2–5 chapters
▨ 5 or more chapters

Source: Data from Upsilon of Kappa Alpha

the Confederate South, just as the cultural South extends well beyond the domain of the old plantation system.

Regional Institutions

Regional institutions play a part in sustaining the South as both idea and reality, tying the region together economically and socially and contributing to a sense of distinctiveness and solidarity. Here, again, we find a close analogy with American ethnic groups. Like some of those groups, the South has its own social and professional organizations, organs of communication, colleges and universities, and so forth. In fact, it probably has more of them now than ever before. When Karl Marx said scornfully of the Confederacy that it wasn't a nation at all, just a battle cry, he was referring to the absence of this sort of institutional apparatus, and until recently the South couldn't *afford* much in the way of regional institutions.

FIGURE 20. *"Dixie" Listings as Percentage of "American" Listings in Telephone Directories, ca. 1975*

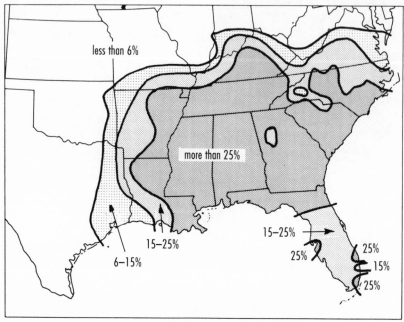

Source: J. S. Reed, "The Heart of Dixie: An Essay in Folk Geography," *Social Forces* 54 (June 1976): 932.

But now the Southern Historical Association, the Southern Railway, the Southern Baptist Convention, the Southern Growth Policies Board, and other, similar institutions establish channels of communication and influence within the region, making it more of a social reality than it would be otherwise. At the same time, even the names of such organizations serve to reinforce the idea that the South exists, that it means something, that it is somehow a fact of nature.

Southern Living magazine, for instance, implies month after month that there is such a thing as Southern living and that it is different and (by plain implication) better. Figure 22 shows where that message falls on fertile ground. Notice that Floridians are relatively uninterested in it. So are Texans, despite heroic efforts by the magazine (including a special southwestern edition). Here we see plainly a development that regional sociologists were

FIGURE 21. *Average Scores on "Index of Southern Preference," 1957*

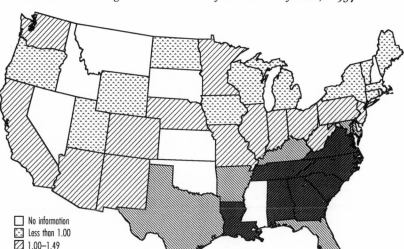

No information
Less than 1.00
1.00–1.49
1.50–1.99
Over 2.00

Source: J. S. Reed, *The Enduring South: Subcultural Persistence in Mass Society* (Chapel Hill: University of North Carolina Press, 1974), 18.
Note: One point each is awarded for liking a Southern accent, liking Southern cooking, and thinking Southern women are better looking than women from elsewhere in the United States.

predicting fifty years ago, something that maps of regional culture and regional identification only hint at: the bifurcation of the South into a "Southeast" centered on Atlanta and a "Southwest" that is, essentially, greater Texas. (Texas has its own magazines.)

We find a similar pattern when we look at one of the South's regional universities. The University of North Carolina at Chapel Hill has long been a center for the study and nurture of Southern culture. It has also helped to educate a regional elite. Figure 23 shows the states in which an appreciable percentage of all college graduates are Chapel Hill alumni. Tar Heels are thick on the ground throughout the southeastern states, but (aside from some brain drain to the New York City suburbs) that's the only place they're thick on the ground. In particular, Chapel Hill has little market penetration west of the Mississippi. (Texas has its own universities.)

FIGURE 22. Southern Living *Readers as Estimated Percentage of White*
Population, 1981

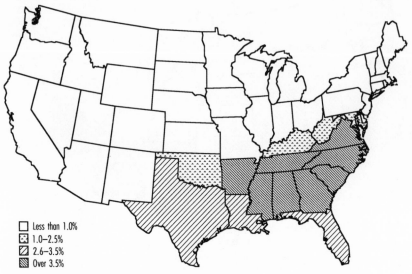

☐ Less than 1.0%
▨ 1.0–2.5%
▨ 2.6–3.5%
▨ Over 3.5%

Source: Data from Marketing Department, *Southern Living*

So Where Is It?

So where is the South? Well, that depends on which South you're talking
about. Some places are Southern by anybody's reckoning, to be sure, but at
the edges it's hard to say where the South is because people have different
ideas about *what* it is. And most of those ideas are correct, or at least useful,
for one purpose or another.

The South is no longer the locus of a distinctive economic system, export-
ing raw materials and surplus population to the rest of the United States
while generating a variety of social and economic problems for itself. That
system is gone, and good riddance. Some of its effects still linger, though,
and a few—such as a substantial black minority population—will be with us
for the foreseeable future. The South is also set apart by its people and their
distinctive ways of doing things. Mass society has made some inroads, but

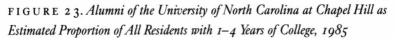

FIGURE 23. *Alumni of the University of North Carolina at Chapel Hill as Estimated Proportion of All Residents with 1–4 Years of College, 1985*

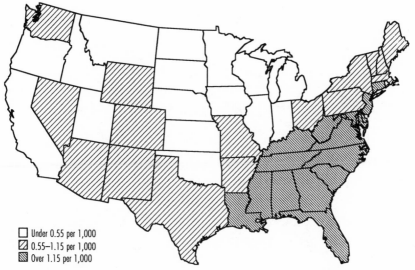

☐ Under 0.55 per 1,000
▨ 0.55–1.15 per 1,000
▩ Over 1.15 per 1,000

Source: Data from Alumni Office, University of North Carolina at Chapel Hill

Southerners still do many things differently. Some are even inventing new ways to do things differently. And the persistence of the cultural South doesn't require that Southerners stay poor and rural. Indeed, poor folks can't afford some of the newest South's trappings—bass boats and four-wheel drives, for instance.

Because its history and its culture are somewhat different from the run of the American mill, the South also exists as an idea—an idea, moreover, that people can have feelings about. Many are fond of the South (some even love it); others have been known to view it with disdain. In either case, the South exists in people's heads and in their conversation. From this point of view, the South will exist for as long as people think and talk about it, and as for its boundaries—well, the South begins wherever people agree that it does.

Finally, the South is a social system, perhaps more now than ever before. A network of institutions exists to serve it, and an ever-increasing number of

FIGURE 24. *"Southern" Listings as Percentage of "American" Listings in Telephone Directories, ca. 1975*

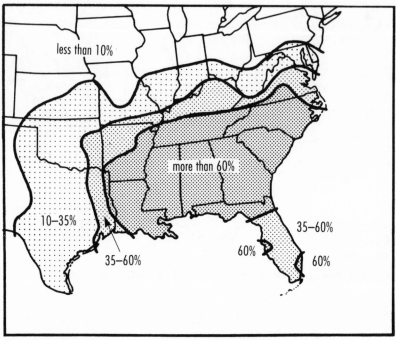

Source: J. S. Reed, "The Heart of Dixie: An Essay in Folk Geography," *Social Forces* 54 (June 1976): 929.

people have a crass, pecuniary interest in making sure that it continues to exist. In this respect, the brute facts of distance and diversity conspire to reduce the South to a southeastern core.

Given all these different Souths, obviously we can't just draw a line on a map and call it the South's border. As Southerners are fond of saying: It depends. But, what the hell, if I had to do it, my candidate would be the line in figure 24 that shows where "Southern" entries begin to be found in serious numbers in urban telephone directories (35–60 percent). The South defined by that line makes a lot of sense. It includes the eleven former Confederate states, minus all but the eastern edge of Texas. It takes in Kentucky, which had a wishful star in the Rebel flag, but not Missouri, which did, too. A corner of Oklahoma makes it in as well: we get Muskogee.

Figure 24 shows variation within the South that also makes sense. It follows some of the stress lines we've already identified. Kentucky and much of Virginia, East Texas and part of Arkansas, most of peninsular Florida—all of these areas on the edges of the South are less "Southern" than the regional heartland, by this measure as by others we've examined. On the other hand, a Southern sphere of influence takes in Maryland, West Virginia, Oklahoma, much of greater Texas, and the southern parts of states from Ohio west to Missouri. Few would include most of these areas in the South proper, but even fewer would deny their Southern cultural flavor.

This one statistic indicates the presence of the sort of regional institutions I mentioned earlier, as well as the kind of regional enthusiasm that leads an entrepreneur to call a newsstand, say, the "Southern Fruit and News." It shows where the idea of the South is vital, where its social reality extends, or both. In other words, if you want to know whether you're in the South, you could do worse than to look in the phone book.

CHAPTER THREE

"The South" and "the Negro"
The Rhetoric of Race Relations and Real Life

NELL IRVIN PAINTER

For Americans born before the 1960s, the very phrase *the South* connects directly to notions of ignorance and violence, usually focused around the enormous and central problem of race. Such connotations grow out of the region's long history of racial oppression, which in the modern era was summed up in the system of racial segregation. The era of legal segregation lasted from about 1890 to the early 1970s, although at the time it seemed to go on forever, defining so much of what we think of as uniquely Southern. Today most Southerners are pleased that the times have changed, for segregation entailed great fear, hypocrisy, and humiliation on both sides of the color line. Desegregation has brought more freedom of thought and association and a new flexibility of identity. Southerners no longer have to range themselves implacably in the two mutually exclusive categories of black and white. Desegregation has allowed whites to forge new, more honest friendships with black equals, and blacks are staking out their claims in the region's history.

Were this a sufficient characterization of the desegregated South, the region would be sunny indeed. But a good deal more remains to be said, for the past is neither forgotten nor done with. Habits of thought and being persist, including the contrast between "the South," on the one hand, and "the Negro," on the other. In this essay I will discuss these entities, the stock-in-trade of the rhetoric of race relations, then turn to the real-life originality of Southern black people.

"The South," "the Negro," and the Rhetoric of Race

In collections of essays about the South produced during the era of segregation, it was customary to include one piece on blacks—only one. After this one nod toward nonwhites, all further discussion of the various aspects of Southern society read as though the South were lily-white, as though Southerners were white by definition. Even though we have improved lately, the attraction of a monolithic black South lingers, and it remains difficult to integrate black writers into discussions of Southern literature and to include the work of black social scientists in histories of Southern social thought. In this anthology I am straddling old and newer ways of thinking about the South. In one essay I must say everything to be said in this book about black Southerners, which is a shadow of the old singular formula of "the Negro." At the same time, I must recognize the complicated history of the people who have made up about one-third of the population of the South. I will speak here of the fictive, monolithic entity defined by race as well as of selected aspects of black Southern history.

During the era of segregation, discussions of Southern society involved two categories that did not overlap: "the South" and "the Negro." *The South* meant white people, and *the Negro* meant black people; both phrases appeared always in the singular and packed with unstated significance. *The South* meant the polity, the economy, the powerful institutions of the region, summed up in the persons of elite whites whose ancestors had owned slaves (lots of them) and who had wholeheartedly supported the Confederacy. *The South* did not mean the impoverished and uneducated white masses whose racial identity had to be qualified with the economic (and moral) designation of "poor." *The South* did not embrace whites who supported the Union in the Civil War or those who later disliked or opposed segregation.

As if to balance the economic symmetry of meaning, *the Negro* carried the unstated connotations of poor, rural, and unschooled. Blacks who did not fit this description also needed some sort of modification to their racial designation, such as "middle-class" or "educated." Within these silent conventions, white Southern writers analyzed their region, as in John Crowe Ransom's leading essay in the influential 1930 anthology, *I'll Take My Stand: The South and the Agrarian Tradition by Twelve Southerners*: "The South is unique on this continent for having founded and defended a culture which was according to the European principles of culture; and the European principles had better look to the South if they are to be perpetrated in this country."

By "European principles," Ransom meant tranquil stability as a good thing, which only made sense from the point of view of someone who was not oppressed. Even Wilbur J. Cash's 1941 classic, *The Mind of the South*, which is still read as truth by many, speaks of *the South* as opposed to *the Negro*.

Such usage considerably simplified the analysis of Southern society by identifying classes with race, although Cash spoke of two classes of whites in his category of *the South*, which helps explain the continuing attractiveness of his text. By defining economically oppressed whites out of society—disappearing them, so to speak—articulate white Southerners managed to erect a stylized construct of Southern society that seemed appealing. A string of million-dollar movies about the Old South, for example the classic favorites *Birth of a Nation* and *Gone with the Wind*, venerated plantation aristocrats who ruled over a society made up principally of people like them and their servants. Despite the allure of the made-up South of popular culture, the reality was harsher and more complicated.

Racism and Class Oppression

From the eighteenth through much of the twentieth century, educated Southerners, the overwhelming majority of whom were white, enjoyed the benefits of life at the top of a society in which many workers were either enslaved or otherwise economically fettered by racist traditions and low wages, and in which there was little need to share political power, especially office holding, with the poor. Stripped down to its bare essentials, such a system violated the democratic principles said to be characteristic of the United States. Racism made the absence of democracy in the South acceptable, even attractive, to most Americans.

Race justified and obscured ordinary class oppression in the United States, even though anyone who thought about the situation realized that the republican ideal of economic mobility was impossible for a working class that was enslaved. Racism allowed Americans of African descent to be counted out—out of the polity, even out of society. The *Dred Scott* decision of 1857, holding that no blacks, slave or free, could be citizens, generalized an idea that had been gaining impetus nationally since the 1830s.

Few Americans realized that, in barring a race from citizenship, they thereby also conveniently silenced the very poor. In the past and today, nearly all black people work for a living and, as a group, represent the nation's poorest people. The habit stuck of dealing with economic and political inequities in terms of race, for as Southerners and as Americans we still speak easily of racial differences while stumbling over matters of economic class.

By thinking in terms of race without seeing class, Southerners distorted (and still distort) discussions of labor relations and class conflict. Instead of phrasing the question in terms of employers and employees, Southerners engaged in the murky discourse of race relations, in which the attributes of race could be both irrational and yet supposedly immutable. Almost anything could be said about race and be believed. Educated white men all could be termed natural leaders who, slim and elegant, were excellent horsemen. Speaking of the monolithic "the Negro," elite Southerners could claim: before the Civil War, that enslaved workers were happy to work for nothing; after the war, that much of the Southern working class was dying out as a consequence of having been emancipated; at the turn of the twentieth century, that raping white women was a racial trait; and, in the 1950s, that because they were black, large numbers of Southerners did not want to exercise ordinary civil rights. Racism made such generalizations seem credible when they were applied to blacks, although they would have seemed ludicrous if spoken about other people.

During the era of segregation, the introduction of race into any discussion

sent most Southern whites into pig-headed denial, as they performed extraordinary (and often unconscious) mental gymnastics to excuse the immo-
bilization and oppression of a large portion of the Southern working class.
White supremacists gained a wide audience in the South that seldom challenged their fantasies, which so often involved sex: an insistence on racial
purity that ignored white men's abuse of black women; a confusion of voting
rights with miscegenation; a stigmatization of black women for their supposed lack of feminine virtues; and hysteria over black male autonomy and
sexuality. Racism also created grotesque stereotypes that delighted whites
and humiliated blacks—and not only in the South. Mammies, Samboes,
Sapphires, Zip Coons, and the rest flourished in American popular culture
for well over a century.

Needless to say, blacks did not accept such degradation silently. At every
turn, they campaigned against defamation, segregation, and lynching. In the
1890s, for instance, blacks boycotted newly segregated streetcars in Jackson-
ville, New Orleans, and other cities. Such journalists as Ida B. Wells of the
Memphis Free Speech challenged white supremacists' explanations of lynching,
with the result that in the mid-1890s her newspaper was destroyed and she
became a refugee in the North. A similar fate befell Atlanta journalist J. Max
Barber in the aftermath of the race riot of 1906.

Any honest evaluation of Southern society must begin by challenging the
scheme that separates "the South" from "the Negro" and then recognize that
the South has long been a multiracial society divided against itself. The
history of race relations is almost uniformly depressing until it reaches the
civil rights era of the mid-twentieth century, for the establishment and maintenance of segregation came at an appalling human cost.

The Southern Black Old Country

Emancipation in 1865 served as the great watershed in race relations (by
making free people of slaves) and black culture (by permitting an increased
level of cultural autonomy). Both processes unfolded during the second half
of the nineteenth and the first half of the twentieth centuries, during the era

of strict racial segregation. Segregation was a repressive response to emancipation, a means of freezing blacks in a subordinate status and preventing the
mobility that had threatened to take place right after 1865. Segregation
represented an entire system of economic, social, and political subjugation.
The "separate but equal" dictum was never any more than a fiction designed
to lend an acceptable rationale to a naked system of oppression. Segregation
consigned blacks—the vast majority of whom were poor—to unskilled work
in agriculture or domestic service. It denied blacks equal protection under
law and barred them from jury service. Segregation posed a threat to the
physical well-being of a black person who contested the will of elite whites by
attempting to vote or trying to collect overdue debts. Segregation kept black
children, most of whom lived in rural areas, in rundown schoolhouses staffed
by underpaid teachers during short terms that were measured in weeks
rather than months.

Schooling was always more tenuous in the countryside than in towns, a
deficiency that was especially hard on black Southerners. Southern blacks
were more rural than Southern whites until about 1960, so that the combination of rurality, poverty, and segregation limited black access to formal education. In 1940, 49 percent of Southern blacks (as opposed to 16 percent of
Southern whites) had completed less than five years of school. By 1960, 32
percent of Southern blacks (and 10 percent of Southern whites) had completed less than five years of school; by 1975, the latest year for which figures
are available, less than 5 percent of both races in the South had no more than
a fifth-grade education.

Racial discrimination and lack of education constricted Southern blacks'
vocational choices, and this limitation affected them with particular severity
because such a large proportion of women were in the work force. On the eve
of the Great Depression, 39 percent of black women and 80 percent of black
men over ten years of age were working for wages, compared to 16 percent of
Southern white women and 75 percent of Southern white men. With the
majority of Southern black men and women employed in agriculture, forestry, fishing, or domestic service, parents were likely to have to work for very
low wages and often to seek work at a distance from their children. This
pattern of low wages persists today, so that families with more than one wage

earner still live in poverty. As late as 1985, 30 percent of African-American families in the South (as opposed to 10 percent of white families and 23 percent of Hispanic families) lived below the poverty level. With 13 percent of its families living in poverty in 1985, the South was still the poorest region in the United States. The median income of Southern black families was $15,800 (for white families, $27,100, and for Hispanic families, $19,000), while the median family income of all American families in 1985 was $27,750. Blacks are still the poorest group in the poorest region of the United States.

Two very important migrations altered Southern black culture. The first occurred when a people who had been mostly Southern began to move to the Northeast and Midwest and, in smaller numbers, into the West. Even though nearly half a million black Southerners left the South between 1870 and 1910, by the latter date more than 90 percent of African Americans still resided in the Southern states. The out-migration gained momentum in the twentieth century, continuing until 1970. In 1980, only 53 percent of blacks lived in the South, but their culture had taken root in the Southern diaspora: St. Louis, Chicago, Oakland, Harlem, and even Minneapolis.

This vast migration resembles Asian, Latin-American, and European immigration to the United States in that black Southern migrants, like immigrants, moved toward economic opportunity and away from social and economic oppression. But one crucial difference separates the experiences of black Southerners from that of immigrants. The latter think of the United States as a promised land and look across the borders to the bad Old Country. But for African Americans, the United States—at least one region of it—represents the oppression they have fled. Having suffered in the land of opportunity, many African Americans feel an ambiguous patriotism that complicates their relationship with their Old Country, the South.

Contemporaneously with that sweeping interregional migration, there occurred a second migration of black Southerners, one that has great importance for this essay: Rural black Southerners moved to town. Whereas 80 percent of African Americans lived in the country in 1890, by 1970 the

Southern black population was only 19 percent rural (compared with 28 percent rural among Southern whites). Between the 1890s and the end of the era of segregation, the move from the country to the city profoundly affected black religion and black music.

The Real Life of Southern Black Music

Few generalizations about Southern society apply to one race but not the other, and the Sanctified movement of the 1890s that created Holiness (or Holy Roller or Pentecostal) churches is no exception. Sanctified churches grew up among whites as well as blacks, just as the radio and the phonographs that spread black gospel music and blues were no respecters of the color line. (This, however, is a history of blacks in the South, not of all Southerners, and the fascinating story of twentieth-century Southern religion as a whole cannot be told here.) The new sacred and secular black Southern music quickly influenced whites as well as blacks, particularly after radios and phonographs became widespread. Both basic types of mid-twentieth-century black music—blues and gospel—have their roots in nineteenth-century religion.

During the antebellum era, most blacks who were slaves either worshiped along with their masters or had no Christian religion. After emancipation, freedpeople formed their own churches, mostly Baptist or Methodist, often as a consequence of the activities of black and white missionaries from such Northern churches as the African Methodist Episcopal Church and the Methodist Episcopal Church, North. Many black Baptists split off from Southern Baptist congregations, causing a crisis in the mother church. Separate churches permitted blacks to elaborate their worship services along African-American lines.

In the nineteenth century, black religion did not include the use of musical instruments. Methodists sang from hymnals based on the songs written and collected by Charles Wesley, brother of John Wesley, the British founder of the Methodist Church. Preferring not to use books, Missionary Baptists and Primitive (meaning fundamentalist) Baptists tended rather to let the preacher line out the long-meter hymns associated with Isaac Watts, a pioneering eighteenth-century English hymn writer associated with Nonconformist religion in Great Britain and the United States. This style of singing, very much rooted in rural life, was called simply "Dr. Watts." It generally began slowly and softly, building melismatically toward a high point during which the congregation would clap or clasp hands. Dr. Watts singing was distinctive in style, employing the African-American full-throatedness, nasal tones, falsetto, and interjection of sounds like growls and moans. This style carried over into new forms of Southern black religion.

The new Holiness churches of the 1890s and the early twentieth century were much more congregation-centered and made much greater use of music and dance than the older churches. Beginning with pianos, tambourines, and drums, Holiness or Sanctified churches have employed ever more elaborate instrumentalization over the years. The most striking aspects of Holiness worship are its rhythmic intensity and the spirit possession of members of the congregation, known as "shouting" or "getting happy." In the 1920s and 1930s the new gospel songs came to be called "Dorseys," after their most prominent creator and performer, Thomas A. Dorsey, to whom I will return below.

The potency of this church-based music derives from its combination of the older traditions of African-American religious singing—Dr. Watts and spirituals—with the rhythms, instruments, and unsentimental evocations of personal realities associated with the blues, which grew out of work songs and field hollers. Gospel music (including quartet singing) and the blues share certain characteristics that distinguish African-American music. Most obvious is the salience and complexity of rhythm. Blues and gospel music also employ a distinctive scale, in which the third, fifth, seventh, and sometimes sixth notes are altered, either lowered or shaded. These are what are called "blue" notes or "bent" tones. The blues are known for a twelve-bar form in which the first line is repeated, a form found in much black gospel music as well. Here are two examples of the twelve-bar blues form:

I am broke and hungry, ragg'd and dirty too.
I am broke and hungry, ragg'd and dirty too.

Mama if I clean up, can I go home with you?[1]

Make your bed up higher, and turn your lamp way low.
Make your bed up higher, and turn your lamp way low.
I'm gonna hug and kiss you, ain't coming here no more.[2]

African-American music is an aural, spontaneous music that cannot be set down and captured once and for all in a written score. Blues and gospel music (like white gospel and country music) are emotional idioms, through which singers aim to involve their audience in a performance that appears unrehearsed and sincere. Black singers use falsetto to increase the emotional punch of the music; they also speak certain lines, growl, moan, and shout to reinforce the felt authenticity of their message. Employing a panoply of techniques, each performer and each performance produces a unique version of familiar songs. This continuing elaboration on a microscopic scale is matched by a long-term evolution of instrumentalization in religious and secular music. Whereas in the nineteenth century, neither work songs nor spirituals were accompanied, twentieth-century blues and gospel music have taken on an ever-enlarging instrumental backup. No matter how elaborate the band, however, the human voice remains the model sound.

Southern black culture remained the fountainhead of creativity for countless singers and pickers who invented and reinvented blues and gospel music. The vast majority of these musicians lived and died in obscurity behind the veil of racial segregation, seldom becoming well known very far outside their own locales. But the professionals who toured and made records gained a wider fame. A handful of prominent performers must stand for the generations of inspirational but unknown bards.

Both W. C. Handy and the pioneer blues singer Gertrude "Ma" Rainey encountered the blues for the first time in the early years of the twentieth century. A native of Columbus, Georgia, Ma Rainey became the first major blues singer, but she did not discover the blues until 1902, when she heard a

1. Jerry Silverman, *One Hundred and Ten American Folk Blues* (New York, 1958), 214–15.
2. Tilford Brooks, *America's Black Musical Heritage* (Englewood Cliffs, N.J., 1984), 55.

young woman singing about the loss of her man. Rainey adopted this poignant style and made her career as a classic blues singer in the 1920s.

W. C. Handy, later known as the "Father of the Blues," was a college-trained musician, born in Alabama, who heard a tired black man accompanying himself on a guitar in a Mississippi train station in 1903. Although the music was not entirely foreign to Handy—he had heard that sort of singing as a boy in Alabama—the overall effect struck him as weird and powerful.

Like gospel singing, blues was at once something old and something new, a twentieth-century novelty that drew on older African-American traditions. Pursuing the invention of the blues leads simultaneously back to Africa and back only as far as 1902. As an old bluesman said of the search for origins: "The blues? Ain't no first blues! The blues always been."[3]

In the absence of phonograph records, tracing the early development of the blues is only possible through personal recollections and sheet music, the latter at best an imprecise gauge of black folk music. Handy's first blues composition was the 1912 "Memphis Blues"; his well-known "St. Louis Blues" was published two years later. Like many other blues and gospel musicians whose names are still known, Handy moved north. He settled in New York in 1918 and continued writing music and the history of black music.

The first blues songs were not recorded until 1920, when "You Can't Keep a Good Man Down" and "This Thing Called Love," by Mamie Smith, were issued in New York. During the 1920s, the best-known performers of classic blues were women, notably Sippie Wallace ("the Texas Nightingale"), Tennessean Bessie Smith, and Ma Rainey ("Mother of the Blues"). Southern born and raised, the stars of the classic blues inevitably migrated from the country, first to Southern and then to Northern cities, and their music differed from what was called the country blues.

Ma Rainey, the first great blues performer, is remembered both for the turbulence of her life and for the originality of her artistry, for as a classic blues singer she incorporated the roughness and spontaneity of Southern

3. Quoted in Eileen Southern, *The Music of Black Americans: A History*, 2d ed. (New York, 1983), 330.

rural (or country) blues. The country blues in the early twentieth century is associated with men like "Texas" Alger Alexander, "Mississippi" John Hurt, "Blind" Lemon Jefferson, and Charlie Patton, whose regional styles varied tremendously. However, country blues singers, who accompanied themselves on guitars, had many techniques in common. They used a raspy, abrasive voice full of falsetto—growling, humming, grunting, and shouting the bent tones and blue notes. Slapping, stomping, and beating, blues performers made themselves and their guitars into percussive instruments.

Singers of the classic blues were more polished and restrained performers, but like country blues artists, they sought to forge links of shared experiences—shared hurts—between themselves and their audiences. A fellow blues singer summed up her memory of Ma Rainey:

> Oh Lord, don't say anything about Ma. All her gold hanging around her tight. Ma was a mess. Ain't nobody in the world ever yet been able to holler "Hey Bo Weevil" like her. Not like Ma. Nobody. I've heard them try to, but they can't do it. "Hey Bo Weevil." All right. 'Cos bo weevil he was eating up everything down South. That worm would eat up all the food and everything. And she holler "Hey Bo Weevil you been gone a long time." Now there was two *meanings* to that. I was such a smart little hip chicken, I knew just which bo weevil she was talking about.[4]

Unattractive by American standards of beauty, Ma Rainey was dark-skinned and full-bodied. Her personal style belonged to old show-business traditions. She had gold teeth and dressed in glittering gowns and diamond tiaras. Rainey straightened her hair and wore light-colored powder, but this did not indicate that she or other women who adopted a similar style wanted to be white. Rainey's persona was rooted in black culture, but as a performer she sought also to convey an impression of wealth and beauty. Expensive clothes straightforwardly advertised her wealth. But the matter of feminine beauty was (and remains) far more ambiguous.

In the United States of the 1920s, the great majority of the population was

---

4. Quoted in Linda Dahl, *Stormy Weather: The Music and Lives of a Century of Jazzwomen* (New York, 1984), 105.

white. Virtually all rich people were white, and, here as elsewhere, the appearance of wealth is much the same as the appearance of beauty. In addition, white people created and manipulated images of beauty, which had partly been fashioned with the color and shape of black women's bodies as negative examples. Two generations before the Black Power and Black-Is-Beautiful movements, Americans, including most blacks, equated lightness with beauty. Like the black entertainers who followed her decades later, Ma Rainey fashioned a black image that preserved the earthiness of black folk culture but adopted the symbols of American beauty—lightness of skin and straightness of hair.

The classic blues singers of the 1920s toured widely in the South but recorded in Chicago or New York, responding to the imperatives of the music industry. The concentration of the recording business in the North and later on the West Coast affected the long-term reputation of Southern artists. The most familiar are those who, like Bessie Smith, recorded in New York. Bessie Smith even made a film. Her fame—particularly vis-à-vis that of Ma Rainey, who recorded in Chicago—reflects as much New York's prominence as a national media center as it does her particular genius and Southern following.

Race records—records produced primarily for the African-American market—brought classic blues singers a national audience, but the blues stars of the 1920s also toured widely with their own bands. Ma Rainey's pianist in the mid-1920s was a talented bluesman known as Barrelhouse Tom or Georgia Tom, Thomas A. Dorsey, who is remembered today as the "Father of Gospel Music."

Born in rural Georgia—his father was a country preacher—Dorsey grew up in Atlanta, where he encountered the various traditions of blues and black church music as well as white revivalists like Billy Sunday. Having spent his youth in the church, Dorsey strayed into the blues and then, in 1921, was converted back into religion. His songwriting model was Charles A. Tindley, a black minister in Philadelphia who wrote favorites like "Stand by Me" that combine the folk images of spirituals and biblical allusions with the emotional intensity of Dr. Watts singing. Though Tindley had earlier made use of blues phrasing by repeating the first line of each verse, it is Dorsey who is remembered for bringing together the two great black musical traditions. Fusing the musical conventions of the blues—notably rhythm and instrumental accompaniment—with the drama and feeling of black Pentecostal religion was Dorsey's great achievement. Long after he had become identified with gospel singing, he admitted that "blues is a part of me, the way I play piano, the way I write."[5]

In 1926 Dorsey wrote the first of what he called gospel songs, "If You See My Savior, Tell Him That You Saw Me." The inspiration for the song came to him in a manner that became typical, from personal experience of illness and lack of money—in short, a blues inspiration. Out of the grief that swept over him after the death of his wife and child in 1932, he wrote his most famous song, "Precious Lord, Take My Hand." Had Dorsey merely composed some one thousand gospel songs, many of which have become favorites among whites as well as blacks, he would be remembered. (He wrote "When I've Done My Best," "Hide Me in Thy Bosom," "Search Me, Lord," and "There'll Be Peace in the Valley," among many others.)

But Dorsey was also a creator of the gospel chorus and the mentor of several talented soloists. He organized the first gospel chorus in 1931, and the following year he founded the National Convention of Gospel Choirs and Choruses together with his longtime collaborator, Sallie Martin. Dorsey also formed a gospel music publishing house.

Dorsey's move to Chicago in the 1910s did not prevent him from touring extensively through the South in the 1920s. But with Dorsey anchored in the Midwest, his protégés, all of whom came from the South, also tended to base themselves in the North. Sallie Martin had her own gospel group during the 1940s and 1950s and published "Just a Closer Walk with Thee." (Martin trained a young gospel pianist who later took the name Dinah Washington, under which she is known as a pioneer of rhythm and blues.) Martin grew up

5. Quoted in Tony Heilbut, *The Gospel Sound: Good News and Bad Times* (New York, 1971), 56.

in a small black settlement in Georgia and as a young adult moved to Atlanta, where she encountered the Holiness church. In the 1920s she and her husband and son migrated to Cleveland and then to Chicago.

Mahalia Jackson, more famous today than Sallie Martin, was another of Dorsey's associates. Jackson's idol in her teenage years was the classic blues singer Bessie Smith, much of whose style Jackson incorporated into her own gospel performances. Jackson migrated from New Orleans to Chicago in 1927. She joined Dorsey in the late 1930s, and he wrote "There'll Be Peace in the Valley" especially for her in 1937. In the late 1940s Jackson launched the recording career that made her famous worldwide. That she has been able to reach nonblack audiences without abandoning gospel music is a testament to the attractiveness of the genre.

The choruses associated with Dorsey and Martin's gospel convention quickly became a national force, one whose impetus came from the South but many of whose best-known artists lived in the Midwest. But another tradition of black church music has remained more firmly rooted in the South: that of gospel quartets. During the same years that the Sanctified movement was laying the groundwork for choral gospel singing, blacks also refined quartet singing into an elaborate form of church-based entertainment. Often the quartets were all male, featuring close harmonies, choreographed movements, and careful dress and grooming.

The formation of the Dixie Hummingbirds in Greenville, South Carolina, in 1929 marks the emergence of a form of Southern black religious music that was related to yet different from gospel choruses. Gospel choruses consisted mostly of women wearing choir gowns and singing with instrumental accompaniment. Gospel quartets might have four or five members and were generally all male. Dressed in matching suits and snapping their fingers to keep time, the quartets initially sang a cappella.

Gospel quartets flourished in the 1940s and prospered well into the 1950s with such groups as the Five Blind Boys of Mississippi, the Soul Stirrers, and the Spirit of Memphis. With their careful, almost mannered choreography, energetic performances, and medley of lead and backup singers, gospel quartets represented a form of entertainment that incorporated ideals from the churches and from the streets. Their carefully tailored suits and "conks" (chemically straightened hair) presented a church-based version of Ma Rainey's image of prosperity and beauty. As with Rainey, one secret of the quartets' success lay in their continuing ability to perform in a spontaneous manner that convinced audiences that the groups knew and shared their troubles.

Like choral gospel music, most quartet singing remained on the amateur level. Singers sought to inspire as well as to entertain their friends and families, so that the line blurred between performer and audience. The use of call and response in African-American music served further to bond singers and listeners into a congregational whole. Gospel quartets, gospel choruses, and blues singers (and, incidentally, country-and-western performers) had to seem to testify and preach through their music, not merely to perform.

Sad and ironic, the blues detailed life's tragedies, whereas gospel soared with the joy of overcoming those same griefs. Closely related in rhythm, scale, and vocal mannerisms, both secular and sacred black music grew out of twentieth-century African-American Southern culture and the segregation that characterized contemporary race relations. Most whites—Northern and Southern—ignored black music until the barriers between the races began to fall after World War II.

White supremacy and strict racial separation had never prevented black and white musicians from borrowing from one another, even in the segregated South. Yet their audiences remained largely distinct well into the twentieth century. The movement away from absolute separation of the races in popular culture had begun first in the North in the 1930s. One example of increased racial flexibility was the series of Carnegie Hall concerts produced by John Hammond in 1938 and 1939, entitled "From Spirituals to Swing." These concerts introduced black musicians—blues singers, gospel groups, and jazz players, most of them Southern—to largely white New York audiences. By the mid-1950s, though Southern life remained segregated, blues and gospel music were making their way into nonblack American culture with rhythm and blues, rock 'n' roll, and jazz. By the 1960s, artists who had hitherto performed on the "chickenbone" circuit—such as Mississippian B. B. King—were performing before white audiences. Aretha Franklin, whose voice and style are filled with the gospel sound of her Mississippi-born preacher father, became an international star, while groups like the Temptations and the Spinners adopted the sounds and mannerisms of the gospel quartets. White performers like Elvis Presley recorded Dorsey's gospel songs, including "Precious Lord, Take My Hand," and American popular music of all sorts employed African-American rhythms full of the intensity and drama of gospel phrasing. The period after the 1950s witnessed the Americanization of Southern black music purely as entertainment.

Present-day American popular music, from rock to country to soul, is deeply indebted to a Northern, urbanized version of what, at midcentury, was mostly black and Southern. Although today's popular music gets its infusion of African rhythms via Jamaica as well as Mississippi, the influence of Southern-based blues and gospel styles is still pronounced. With the migration of millions of blacks to cities outside the South, these other places now figure largely in the map of African-American culture. Compared with the recorded popular music of the first half of this century, new black musical forms like rap and disco owe relatively little to the South. At the same time, the crumbling of racial barriers has made it easier for whites to present themselves as performers of black music.

The Civil Rights Era

Something else was going on at the same time that white Americans (and Britons) were discovering and appropriating Southern black music. African Americans were also casting off the timidity and otherworldliness that had protected communities of preachers and their congregations during the worst of the segregation era. Much that affected black Americans changed during and after World War II: unionization, the March on Washington movement, military service and the desegregation of the military, and increased migration out of the South.[6]

In a postwar world in which colored nations were becoming independent and Soviets criticized Americans for racism, the imperatives of empire and the Cold War discouraged parochial habits like white supremacy. Foreign as well as domestic politics contributed to the watershed 1954 U.S. Supreme Court decision, *Brown* v. *Board of Education*, which struck down racial segregation in public schools and signaled the end of segregation in Southern public life. Other decisions prohibited the white primary and poll taxes, means by which Southern states had disfranchised the mass of black voters. But these changes did not become manifest in the South until black Southerners—most of them associated with churches, often the very churches that had nourished the magnificent tradition of gospel choirs and quartets—took to the streets to demonstrate against racial oppression.

The civil rights movement of the 1950s and 1960s profoundly altered Southern society and affected many aspects of black identity. On the one hand, the movement galvanized Southern blacks and utilized the racial solidarity created by white supremacy. The Southern Christian Leadership Conference (SCLC), in particular, was able to build the unity implicit in the formula "the Negro" into a potent force for change. On the other hand, the civil rights movement's very success in dismantling the political, economic, and social structure of segregation also undermined black solidarity based strictly on race.

The modern civil rights movement began in 1955 in Montgomery, Alabama, in what Alabama's license plates call the heart of Dixie. Beginning as a protest against the rough handling of black women by bus drivers, inflexible Jim Crow seating arrangements on public transportation, and a lack of jobs for blacks, the Montgomery bus boycott lasted a year. The boycott led to the

6. Between 1940 and 1950, 1,599,000 black Southerners left the South; from 1950 to 1960, 1,473,000; and from 1960 to 1970, 1,380,000.

formation of the organization that became SCLC and propelled a young preacher from Atlanta, the Reverend Martin Luther King, Jr., into national prominence.

King's talents were many. He was articulate, well educated, and in command of the idioms of Southern black religious culture. His ability to inspire people who had thought themselves powerless was virtually unique. Through organization and inspiration, King and SCLC brought the Southern black churchgoing masses into the streets and the county offices to protest the Southern racial status quo. The protests—the whole movement, in fact— made use of the music of Southern black churches.

The attempt to register poor Southern blacks as voters was the special task of a coalition of organizations led by the Student Nonviolent Coordinating Committee (SNCC), which was formed, at the behest of SCLC's Ella Baker, at a 1960 conference held at Baker's alma mater, Shaw University in Raleigh, North Carolina. Northern and Southern students (now middle-aged) who participated in the Freedom Summer of 1964 think of SNCC as "the movement," seared as they were by the murderous violence that white supremacists were willing to commit. For SNCC volunteers, the 1964 murder of three civil rights workers near Philadelphia, Mississippi, was the great example of how far white supremacists would go to forestall black civil rights. Freedom Summer attracted large numbers of white students, and two of the three Philadelphia victims were white Northerners, which meant that the killings attracted wide media coverage. White newspapers and television had, however, ignored the hundreds of Southern blacks who had been beaten and murdered during the preceding decade in pursuit of the vote.

For the Southern black masses—the people who went to church and sang gospel music or who stayed away from church and sang the blues—the campaigns that SCLC mounted over the years were more important than Freedom Summer. In cities like Albany, Georgia, Birmingham and Selma, Alabama, and Memphis, Tennessee, SCLC organized mass protests aimed at wresting political power away from traditional elites and increasing blacks' access to jobs.

SCLC, SNCC, and the whole civil rights movement persuaded Congress to pass the landmark legislation of the mid-1960s, but an even more immedi-

ate and sensational goad to lawmakers was the nonviolent Birmingham campaign of 1963—with an assist in the same year from the huge, peaceful,
interracial March on Washington for Jobs and Freedom, led by a coalition of
civil rights, religious, and labor organizations. By 1963 SCLC had realized
the wisdom of exploiting the violence of white supremacists, who were un-
mindful of the awful spectacle they presented on nationwide television.
Skillfully manipulated by SCLC, media coverage presented starkly contrast-
ing images. Churchgoing, nonviolent black protesters marched, prayed, and
sang the intensely moving gospel music they had created over the years.
Their adversaries appeared as irrational, bloody-minded bigots bent on re-
fusing upstanding Christians their ordinary citizens' rights, merely because
of their color. The rightness of the peaceable black cause and the ugliness of
white-supremacist violence pressured Congress to pass the Civil Rights Act
of 1964, the most far-reaching piece of civil rights legislation in this nation's
history.

SNCC volunteers performed invaluable services in Mississippi: register-
ing blacks to vote, setting up freedom schools, and involving oppressed
people in community activities that had seemed forbidden before. In an
unofficial freedom vote organized by a coalition of civil rights organizations in
1963, 80,000 disfranchised Mississippi blacks dared to cast votes for the also
unofficial Mississippi Freedom Democratic party (MFDP), which sent a
delegation headed by Fannie Lou Hamer to the Democratic nominating
convention of 1964. The MFDP did not succeed in gaining seats at the
convention, but the freedom vote proved beyond a shadow of a doubt that
white-supremacist rhetoric about blacks' lack of interest in voting was no
more than a tissue of lies. In the following year, SCLC organized a march for
the right to vote from Selma to Montgomery, Alabama; the march provoked
police violence that was captured on national television. By the time it ended,
the protest at Selma had garnered nationwide support, and celebrities flew in
from all over the country to join the march for voting rights.

Congress responded to all this positive and negative pressure by passing
the Voting Rights Act of 1965, which provided for federal oversight of
elections and a series of safeguards in areas where large proportions of the
electorate had been disfranchised. After 1965 Southern blacks began to

register and vote, creating a revolution in Southern politics that faltered during the Reagan years but has not ended. These changes can easily be traced in Mississippi.

After 1964 the MFDP divided seats at Democratic nominating conventions with the officially recognized but lily-white Mississippi Democratic party until the mid-1980s, when the two parties merged. In 1986 Mississippi voters elected Michael Espy as their first black congressman since Reconstruction. Espy's election depended on the votes of many whites, but without the Voting Rights Act of 1965, blacks might never have cast the votes that made Espy's election feasible.

The civil rights movement of 1955–65, which was marked by popular participation in nonviolent demonstrations, revolutionized Southern society in numerous ways both subtle and obvious. Certainly the participants entertained very high hopes for what the movement could achieve, and certainly its results fell short of their expectations. But just as segregation was a system of racial subjugation with social, economic, and political ramifications, so the changes wrought by the civil rights movement, still unfolding, are many and varied. The most pronounced shift has been from a concentration on access to public accommodations and the vote to an overwhelming concern for jobs. This is primarily a change of emphasis, for even in the early 1960s the demand was for "jobs and freedom." Martin Luther King, Jr., embodied this shift. Having begun his public life with a protest against segregated city buses, he died showing solidarity with striking sanitation workers.

Desegregation and Reaction

In retrospect, the most salient section of the Civil Rights Act of 1964 has been Title VII, which prohibits discrimination on account of race (and sex) by employers and unions. This provision has made it possible for workers, usually with the help of such civil rights organizations as the National Association for the Advancement of Colored People (NAACP), to sue unions or employers for the right to employment or to advancement on the job. For Southern black workers, this has meant breaking out of the narrow spectrum of "Negro" jobs and advancing along lines of seniority that previously had been limited to whites.

In three Southern industries—steel (Birmingham, Alabama, and Baltimore, Maryland), tobacco (Virginia and North Carolina), and textiles (North Carolina, South Carolina, and Georgia)—black workers have successfully sued their unions and their employers for equal access to employment and promotion. With the exodus of white men from these fields into relatively high-paying new areas of industrial employment in the South, black workers since the late 1960s have found increased opportunities in manufacturing. The textile industry, long a white preserve, clearly reflects these changes.

In 1966, before the Equal Employment Opportunity Commission (created by the Civil Rights Act of 1964) began monitoring the textile industry's compliance with Title VII, blacks—clustered in janitorial positions—represented only 8 percent of the work force in textiles. By 1968, however, black workers had increased their participation in the textile work force to 13 percent, which included semiskilled jobs as operatives that they had hitherto not been allowed to hold. By the early 1970s, the Southern textile industry was overwhelmingly female and, depending on the plant, anywhere from 25 to 85 percent black. In Georgia, South Carolina, and North Carolina in 1978, 26 percent of all jobs in textiles were held by blacks. About one-third of the black workers were operatives, but only a handful were employed in salaried positions. Even today black women are rarely employed as secretaries in the textile (or any other Southern) industry.

In the late 1960s, black women eagerly moved into semiskilled positions in the textile industry from even lower-paying jobs as waitresses or domestic servants. Unlike many of their white predecessors, black textile workers did not come to the factory directly from agriculture, and they were less susceptible to employer paternalism than white workers had been. This distinction has encouraged the unionization of Southern industries that employ large numbers of blacks—particularly textiles, which long resisted unionization.

Since the 1960s, when black workers, many of whom were highly religious, married their church affiliation to the civil rights movement, black workers have been willing to use collective means to achieve economic and social betterment; they are therefore sympathetic to unions. Many black Southern

workers see the campaign for economic empowerment through union organization as an extension of the struggle for civil rights—the one depending on
racial solidarity, the other on class solidarity. While many Southern whites
remained wary of collective action in the 1960s and 1970s, blacks embraced
mass action, which the civil rights movement had shown to be effective in the
pursuit of poor people's rights. In the Oneita mills in South Carolina and the
J. P. Stevens mills in North Carolina, for instance, the enthusiastic support of
black workers produced union victories.

The consequences of changes as fundamental as those wrought by the civil
rights movement are bound to be complicated, even conflicting on some
levels. After more than twenty years, understandably, various black Southerners define racial interests differently, as the legacies of federal legislation
indicate. The Civil Rights Act made it possible for African-American workers in the South to enter industrial jobs that were more likely to be unionized
than were domestic and agricultural work, and labor organization, in turn,
built upon and reinforced the civil rights movement's evocation of racial
solidarity. At the same time, however, the political ramifications of the Voting
Rights Act demonstrate the potential for racial fragmentation. An example
from the Deep South illustrates this point.

Ordinarily the Alabama Black Belt vote fraud cases of 1985 are taken as an
indication of the Reagan administration's hostility toward independent black
political power, which is a correct reading of the national import of these
trials. Briefly stated, the U.S. Justice Department tried for vote fraud several
black defendants who had been prominent civil rights activists, the best
known of whom was Albert Turner. A close associate of the Reverend Martin
Luther King, Jr., in the 1960s and an SCLC leader in Alabama, Turner had
marched in King's cortege in 1968.

In the mid-1980s Turner and his associates achieved a measure of political
success by pledging themselves to support the interests of the people of the
Alabama Black Belt, the majority of whom were poor and black. Ranged on
the other side were black politicians who favored accommodation with the
local power structure; they reasoned that cooperation with those who had
long wielded economic and political power was simply good strategy.

Even though all the accusers and all but one of the defendants in the vote fraud trials were black, media coverage tended to portray the struggle in racial terms—Turner and his allies representing the black side, their opponents, the white side—because the powerful people in Alabama and in the Justice Department were not black. That Turner and his colleagues were continuing the civil rights tradition of representing the poor reinforced this dichotomy. The outcome of the trials—acquittal on all but minor charges—was seen as a black victory, considering that the defendants had good civil rights credentials and the support of black organizations. Although this was the proper conclusion from the vantage point of recent history, it obscures the interesting point that, in the Alabama Black Belt, blacks had disagreed on what, exactly, constituted their best interests. These disagreements were over ideological and economic issues that cannot be sorted out unequivocally according to race alone.

If the significance of race declines in Southern public life, African Americans may be expected more and more to diverge ideologically and therefore politically. But as long as the poor in the South continue to be disproportionately black and as long as racial discrimination remains a reality, politics in the South will display a black side and a white side. In the meantime, one thing is clear. The breakup of the rigid system of white supremacy and the end of the era of segregation have made discussions of "the Negro" meaningless.

Black Southerners as Southerners

Much has changed since midcentury, but much, particularly in rural areas, remains the same, because economic power remains entrenched among white elites. Throughout most of the South, especially the urban South, blacks have begun to exercise their civil rights in a political revolution that continues to unfold. The mounting influx of non-Southerners, many of whom are Hispanic, Asian, or Jewish, makes it impossible to go on generalizing about Southern society as biracial and culturally monolithic. The modern South differs from that of fifty years ago, in large part because black Southerners (like white Southerners) have been leaving home in extraordinary numbers. Especially in the once heavily populated Deep South, this exodus has altered the region's human geography. For black Southerners, interestingly enough, the human tide turned between 1975 and 1980, when only 220,000 black Southerners left the region and 415,000 blacks moved into the South from other regions.

The cultural repercussions of black migration out of the South have been national, even international in scope. Over the course of the twentieth century, the blues, jazz, and gospel music have become widely recognized idioms, many of whose present-day practitioners are neither Southern nor black. No matter what their race or the region in which they live, today's Americans are more likely than ever to be acquainted with some aspects of the culture that black Southerners created. And thanks to the civil rights movement, non-Southerners in the South are likely to encounter Southern blacks in virtually all aspects of public life—as highway patrolmen, bank tellers, ward heelers, and mayors—which would have been virtually unheard of as recently as the 1960s. In its various guises, much racism remains in the South, as it does in other American regions. But black Southerners are far more able to share their strengths as artists, workers, and thinkers than ever before.

One symbol of the new age is black Southerners' increasing willingness to claim the South as their own territory and a sometimes begrudging, often delighted willingness on the part of white Southerners to acknowledge this claim. The best-known example of this reclaiming occurs in eastern North Carolina on the Somerset plantation, where descendants of several slave families have convened each Labor Day since 1986. Inspired by Dorothy Spruill Redford, who traces her heritage back to the enslaved workers of Somerset, the African Americans whose ancestors built an empire now insist that their contribution be recognized. Southern history, as well as the Southern future, must take its black side into account.

Urbanization in a Rural Culture
Suburban Cities and Country Cosmopolites

D A V I D   R.   G O L D F I E L D

Soft summer evenings punctuated by the distant tinkling of a piano, the muffled clatter of dinner dishes, and the chatter of crickets. This was and still is the urban South, a landscape of open windows and front porches framed by wisteria, crepe myrtle, and oak. It is a landscape that seems far removed from the glitzy office towers or the comfortable resort communities that have become the standard contemporary depictions of the urban South. But appearances are often deceptive in the South. It is a land of indirection, and its cities, for all their anonymous architecture, share in that deception. Southern cities are offsprings of the Southern countryside: until very recently, most of their people came from rural areas and brought with them, as did European immigrants to Northern cities, their cultural baggage.

The rural heritage of the urban South is evident in ways often taken for granted. Most migrants from outside the region have come from another metropolitan area, most likely a suburb. They fit into the Southern urban environment comfortably because the Southern city is really a suburb. It is half as dense as cities elsewhere in the country, and easy annexation laws have enabled it not only to retain its low density but to sprawl out on the landscape to the point where rural and urban spill into and out of each other. Growing up in the age of the automobile and unencumbered by the dinosaur remains of heavy industry, the Southern city has skipped happily along, devouring space and meandering in a seemingly aimless pattern wherever the highways take it.

Aside from their blend of rural and urban—a middle landscape, if you will—Southern cities, for all their self-styled sophistication, still move to a rural beat. The seasons have great meaning in the urban South—not so much for the climate, but for what they imply. Take a walk through any Southern city or town in the spring, and the careful attention to landscaping and planting become evident in the riot of colors that adorn the neighborhoods. "Beauty Is Our Money Crop" was the motto of a fictional Georgia town in a Flannery O'Connor short story, but the phrase is applicable with equal justification to any Southern town. Cities celebrate the spring with festivals, home and garden tours, and general obeisances to local flora. If cotton once was the most characteristic plant of a rural-dominated society, then perhaps the azalea is the symbol of the modern South. And if the spring is a time of energy in the urban South, the summer is a period of languor. Wardrobe departments have traditionally twiddled their thumbs when their theater companies put on Tennessee Williams's plays; Stanley Kowalski's torn T-shirt in *A Streetcar Named Desire* was less for sex appeal than for functionality. Although air-conditioning has taken the edge off the heat and humidity, Southern cities still operate at slower paces during the summer.

These rural carryovers are not at all surprising, considering that migrants from the rural South originally peopled Southern cities. Newer Southern residents may have come from a major metropolitan area of the Northeast or Midwest or even from a European city. Among the major characteristics of life in these cities is ethnic diversity: politics, occupations, civic events, and recreations all have their ethnic dimensions. There are Italians, Poles, and Jews in Southern cities as well. In fact, Charleston was the center of Judaism in colonial America. But the proportion of ethnics in Southern cities dwindled in the nineteenth century, especially after the Civil War. Some historians have maintained that the presence of cheap black labor discouraged white immigration. Although there may be some truth in this argument, the basic fact is that the South was a poor region. Immigrants sought the main chance, and that chance lay elsewhere in the country. So, instead of ethnic divisions in the urban South, racial and class distinctions are what count. Southerners, ever conscious of doing the "right" thing, know about the "right" clubs, the "right" schools, and the "right" law firms. They also know about black and white. A different etiquette operated with respect to race. Slavery and subservience before the Civil War and segregation and deference after 1865 characterized the public interaction between black and white, an interaction designed to underscore the superiority of one race over another.

Southern urban residents also take their religion very seriously. This does not imply that people in the rest of the world are any less righteous. But it is a fact that Southerners are the most churchgoing people in the country. Piety is infectious, because even migrants to the region fall into the pattern of regular church or synagogue attendance. Churches are also prominent physical focal points in their respective communities. This central role of religion in Southern urban life reflects again the rural heritage of the population. The evangelical denominations—Baptists, Methodists, and Presbyterians, in particular—came south to the forest clearings in the early nineteenth century, bringing the gospel to a generally unchurched people. When the people began moving to the cities, so did the churches. Today the flagship churches of these denominations are located in Southern cities, and some call Nashville the Protestant Vatican because it is the headquarters of a vast religious publishing empire and the seat of the Southern Baptist Convention. The fact that religious metaphors and biblical phrases slip into daily conversations and patterns of speech reflects the blurred line between religious and secular that has characterized Southern life since the nineteenth century.

In the same way, the demarcation between public and private is also unclear. For the longest time, a relatively small group of businessmen and professionals have run Southern cities. Though the political situation is more open today, there is still a sense in many places that the chamber of commerce's agenda is synonymous with the general welfare. And in providing services, Southern cities have usually followed the instincts of their rural forebears and left most of those activities to individuals or to private agencies. Low taxes and low services represented more than frugality; they were reflections of Jeffersonian traditions exalting limited government and the independence of the yeoman farmer.

Southern cities are not only logical extensions of the countryside, but they reflect Southern history as well. If the South has been poor in a land of plenty, so have Southern cities; if the South has suffered from its economic dependence on the North, so have Southern cities; if the South has been burdened by white supremacy, illiteracy, and ill health, so have Southern cities; and if the South has elevated its history to folklore and its ancestors to folk heroes, then the same is true of Southern cities. It is not surprising, then, that what one sees, feels, and hears in Southern cities results from a combination of rural culture and regional history, blending in distinctive and often surprising patterns.

Consider the wonderful contradictions: a reverence for the past, yet a penchant for destroying symbols of that past for the sake of the new; a deep, abiding religious faith, yet a seeming indifference to social problems; an emphasis on good manners, indirection in speech, and proper, staid public behavior, yet a loudmouthed, boisterous boosterism without subtlety or sense; an emphasis on individualism, yet a disdain for individual dissent; and a fierce localism, yet a willing dependence on Northern and federal assistance. Of course, the South is replete with ironies. Explaining them or explaining them away have been important ways in which Southern historians have made their livings. But all of these contradictions relate, more or less, to the South's distinctive history. In order to understand the region's cities, it is appropriate to look into that history to find out how these peculiarities came about, how they manifest themselves today, and how they may be transformed in the future.

The First Southern Cities: A Middle Landscape

When Englishmen first began to settle the southern part of what later became the United States, their experience of urban life was brief. The desire and necessity for security and mutual assistance motivated the settlement of Jamestown. But once the colonists began to feel safe and relatively well fed, they wanted to pursue the dream of most Englishmen to own some land. From then on, it was a constant battle for royal authorities to get the Virginians to settle in towns. English officials not only equated urban life with civilization, but they could monitor the colonists' commercial activities much better in a compact settlement than if their subjects were scattered throughout the wilderness. The Virginians held a different perspective, however. With the aid of swiftly flowing rivers that penetrated deep into the interior of the colony and soils that were conducive to the cultivation of a staple crop—tobacco—to which Europeans quickly became addicted, the colonists were doing just fine, thank you, in the countryside. They possessed an almost perverse admiration of their "wild and rambling way," as one planter put it. Those urban places that eventually emerged in the colony were usually administrative centers (such as Williamsburg) or small, local market towns that rarely numbered more than one hundred souls.

This is not to say that all English colonists to the South followed the Virginians' example. But, regardless of where they located, the settlers' longing for the land persisted. In this desire, they were not much different from English colonists elsewhere. It was just that the South offered more opportunities to indulge that penchant. And once Southerners had been drawn into the vortex of a staple economy dependent on vast domains of land and slaves, it became very difficult for them to alter their lifestyles, even if they had wanted to.

The few genuine urban places that appeared during the colonial period in the South reflected this preference for the rural life. Charleston, South Carolina, became the premier colonial Southern city. Despite its size, however, it was a temporary city whose leading citizens moved in and out to the rhythms of the seasons, agricultural cycles, and, above all, the fevers that stalked the Low Country rice plantations. In many respects, they simply moved their country environments to the city, with a few slight modifications necessary for urban living. They created a middle landscape, a distinctive blend of rural and urban. Their town homes (called "single houses") featured long verandas characteristic of their country estates, only turned sideways and extending back into the lot rather than paralleling the street where frontage was expensive. They framed their residences in an abundance of beauty. Copious plantings of flowers and shrubs adorned the courtyards and backyards of their homes. These flourishing gardens walled off urban life; they were sanctuaries from the rattle of carriages on the cobblestones and the cries of commerce along the streets. In the evening, these country gentlemen and their ladies would walk out along the Battery—a promenade by the sea—as much to take in the fresh sea breezes as to socialize and be seen. It was life in andante.

Of course, not everyone in Charleston was a lady or a gentleman, economically speaking. There were middling sorts such as shopkeepers and artisans. But they mostly longed to be transients as well—to own some land, perhaps even a plantation and slaves in the countryside. The country set the standard for the city in architecture, aspirations, and economy. And then there were slaves. Urban slavery seems almost a contradiction in terms, because we associate the institution with the plantation. But slaves were a vital part of Charleston's economy, as artisans, day laborers, and servants. They generally resided near their masters, which gave the city an appearance of residential integration. In fact, well into the twentieth century, at least until urban renewal destroyed many inner-city neighborhoods, it was not unusual to find blacks and whites living near each other.

Propinquity did not breed intimacy, however. It would be a mistake to read anything positive about urban race relations into Southern patterns of residential integration. In Charleston, masters along and near Meeting Street (in the present-day historic district) housed their slaves in two-story structures adjacent to the main house. Slaves resided in small rooms on the top floor, while space in the bottom portion was reserved for horses and carriages. Today these surviving remnants of the Old South often serve as student quarters, with the ground level adapted as parking garages for automobiles.

Savannah offers another Southern colonial example of the countryside brought to town. The creation of English philanthropist James Oglethorpe, it was founded rather late—1733—in the colonial period. The city never approached the social glitter or architectural opulence of Charleston, but it gained widespread notice and admiration for its plan. Oglethorpe, as wary of urban living as any Virginian yet recognizing its necessity for commerce and community, planned "a greene garden Towne," as he called it. His simple grid plan divided the city into four quadrants, each dotted with squares. These were urban oases, where residents and visitors could linger on benches under broad shade trees, surrounded by green. Along the residential streets, Oglethorpe moderated the urban environment (and the climate) by providing large numbers of trees that created arborways rather than thoroughfares.

Charleston and especially Savannah retain their charm today. Though both cities are major ports and are generally prosperous, they have held on to their rural heritage. This retention resulted mainly from the simple fact that, for a large part of the nineteenth century and the beginning of the twentieth, the two towns languished in the backwaters of American civilization. There was no pressure from developers to cast aside the leafy gardens or the generous squares. Residents seemed content to enjoy their past undisturbed by the outside world. Charleston's working motto, according to one observer in 1913, seemed to be "Go away and let me sleep." These cities pioneered "backward chic." When they awoke, the relics of their past had become much more than local curiosities; they were viewed as national treasures, and Americans flocked to see the measure of what they had lost in other parts of the country.

Country Rhythms in City Streets

The languid air of these early Southern cities should not lull us into the idea that they spent most of their time practicing to be museum pieces. Though the countryside continued to call the seasonal tunes of cities in the Old South, urban residents managed numerous improvisations that attracted attention and growth. As the cotton economy prospered, so did Southern cities. Steamboats crowded the wharves of New Orleans, and that city actually surpassed New York as an export center for several years during the 1830s; smokestacks from tobacco factories and iron foundries clouded the skies over Richmond; cotton factors clamored for choice office space in Mobile and Memphis. Though closely tied to the rhythms of agriculture, these cities held aspirations much like cities elsewhere in the country. They eagerly promoted economic development, financed railroads, chartered banks, and expanded the role of local government.

Yet, for all their similarities with cities elsewhere, the urban places of the

South evoked particular responses from travelers who found the environment distinctive. Frederick Law Olmsted, landscape architect and travel writer for a New York newspaper, commented on Richmond's "slovenly appearance" compared with Northern cities of similar size; he used that phrase repeatedly in his descriptions of the urban South. Southern city dwellers seemed to hold fiercely to Thomas Jefferson's dictum: "That government which governs least governs best."

Although the functions of local government expanded during the last few decades before the Civil War, low taxes and modest services continued to characterize the official function in the urban South. The individualistic predilections of agrarian life, modest growth rates, and the interlocking directorate of business and political leaders restricted the extent of revenues raised and services provided. The concept of the general welfare was not a widely held ideal among Southern urban officials, unless that welfare coincided with the enhancing of economic development. City councils in the South paved few streets, offered limited fire and police protection, and provided little in the way of sanitary services outside of the business district. A story that circulated among Southern cities during the 1850s tells of a man who is seen traversing a street waist-deep in mud. Another gentleman hails him from the safety of a wooden sidewalk and asks if he needs help. The mired man responds: "No; but the horse I'm riding sure could."

The condition of Southern streets had its serious side as well. Killing frosts came late to the South, thereby providing an extended breeding season for microorganisms and mosquito larvae. The slovenly cities were not only unsightly, they were unhealthy as well. Yellow fever was the main scourge of the urban South. In 1853 one-sixth of the population of New Orleans succumbed to the disease; in 1855 an epidemic struck Norfolk, Virginia, wiping out a similar proportion of the total population. Though officials tried shooting cannons and lighting torches to ward off the disease, the only effective protection against infection was to escape. Southerners left their cities at the end of May, not returning until the fall. When crops were still in the fields and an epidemic was likely, there was no point in hanging around.

Urban leaders did have a vague idea of what conditions were conducive to yellow fever. When news broke of an epidemic in a neighboring city, a frantic cleanup campaign ensued. Most cities had quarantine laws, but because the implementation of these statutes impeded the flow of trade, the merchant-dominated governments rarely invoked them. Disease control in the urban South, like the provision of services, revolved around the whims and wishes of the business community.

Travelers frequently commented upon the numbers of blacks—slave and free—they encountered in Southern cities. Slaves, they noted, adapted readily to city life. They worked in the tobacco factories of Louisville, in the iron foundries of Richmond, on the railroads in Atlanta, and on the wharves of New Orleans. Urban employers hired rather than purchased many of these slaves since renting did not involve a heavy initial capital outlay. Rent-a-slave services emerged in many Southern cities to accommodate this new demand. Slaves preferred urban work because it enabled them to earn money as bonuses for extra work; they could usually choose their employers and housing arrangements; and, on rare occasions, they were able to save enough money to purchase their freedom.

Had these same travelers been a bit more discerning, they might also have noticed an uneasiness among Southern urban dwellers. During the years between 1840 and 1860, a national economy had emerged that was centered in the Northeast, particularly in New York. Commerce, information, credit, manufactured goods, and wealth all flowed to Gotham for redistribution to its tributaries around the nation. The Mississippi River, once the nation's major commercial highway and the South's economic lifeline, receded in importance, eclipsed by the railroad. As the East drew the West increasingly into its economic orbit, so the South grew dependent on New York as well—for marketing its staple crops and manufactures, for credit, and for shipping. One writer estimated that the South was losing about $133 million annually by 1860 as a result of this dependence.

Southern urban leaders were aware of these events. Coupled with the South's political weakness and the rise of a political party—the Republican—that promised to use the federal government to enhance the economy of Northern cities, the economic situation generated a frenzy of activity during the 1850s. Southern cities went heavily into debt building railroads, constructing factories, and improving wharf and market facilities. These efforts were intended not only to result in great cities, but also to save the South from economic and political subservience. Unfortunately, the scenario did not play out. The 1850s were prosperous years for Southern agriculture, and thus capital and labor gravitated to that sector of the Southern economy, limiting investment opportunities in the cities. Labor shortages plagued the cities as plantation owners called home their slaves. Once again, the Southern city was dancing to a country song.

Cities without Industries and Industries without Cities

The outcome of the Civil War sealed the economic fate of Southern city and region. For nearly a century after Appomattox, Southern cities were way stations to Northern metropolises, ferrying agricultural produce, raw and processed, to markets in the North. The Civil War had demonstrated that, under proper conditions, the South could develop an urban industrial potential. But after the war, in a cash-poor region, cotton was the only commodity that brought a viable price, and Southerners dedicated themselves to its cultivation with a single-mindedness that ultimately beggared black and white, city and farm.

Economic changes and the continued ascendancy of the railroad caused a major shift in the pattern of Southern urbanization during the half-century following the Civil War. The coastal cities—Charleston, Savannah, Mobile, and New Orleans—had been the major urban centers of the Old South. With the postwar decline in water commerce and the long agricultural depression that gripped the region, these cities languished. New Orleans was the fifth-largest city in the country in 1860. By 1900 it had declined to fifteenth. In 1860 Charleston was the third-largest city in the South; by 1910 it was fifteenth.

The nexus of urbanization in the South had shifted to the interior, particularly to an area known as the Piedmont Crescent, a swathe of land that extended south from Richmond; widened to encompass the area between Raleigh and Charlotte in North Carolina; narrowed through Spartanburg, Greenville, and Anderson in South Carolina; continued on through Atlanta;

and culminated in the Appalachian foothills south of what became Birmingham, Alabama. You can locate the major urban places along this crescent today by tracing Interstate 85. The highway follows, more or less, the path of the Southern Railway. The Piedmont provided an ideal topography for the construction of railroad lines. There were few natural barriers, and its soils could support the weight of the tracks and rolling stock. Atlanta became the major railroad terminus for the South during the late nineteenth century. On busy days, the city's various train terminals, in their pace and density, resembled Atlanta's Hartsfield International Airport today, with the major difference that the trains usually ran on schedule.

Atlanta in many ways epitomized the new city of the New South. It was not located on any body of water (though rivals noted its proneness to flooding during heavy rains). But if one draws a line from Chicago to Miami and another line from Boston to New Orleans, they will intersect just around Atlanta. Southern statesman John C. Calhoun noted Atlanta's strategic location as early as 1840. General William T. Sherman was also impressed with the city's location. Postwar boosters hoping to trade on the city's geography quickly rebuilt the railroad network. From these boosters' efforts, Atlanta not only emerged as a regional rail center but also as the spiritual home for the New South Creed—a collection of ideals extolling industrial development, sectional reconciliation, and white supremacy. Atlanta journalist Henry W. Grady became the leading advocate, traveling the breadth of the nation to convince potential investors to put their money into Southern enterprises. His missionary work notwithstanding, about the only portion of the creed that achieved fruition was the part about white supremacy.

This is not to say that Southern cities did not sprout industries during the postwar era. They did; but it was a curious kind of industrialization that did not cause appreciable urbanization. The Piedmont, again, provided the setting for the South's great leap into and even over the industrial age. Railroad connections, the rapid increase in cotton cultivation, a surplus white labor force (the South was the most prolific region in the nation), and the availability of water power combined to make the Southern Piedmont a particularly effective site for the textile industry. Charlotte's D. A. Tompkins was midwife to the industry, coaxing the birth of mills up and down the tracks of the Southern Railway in such towns as Greensboro, Charlotte, Gastonia, Spartanburg, Greenville, and Anderson, as well as numerous smaller towns and new mill villages in between. Tompkins's "Cotton Mill Campaign" was so successful that by 1905 more than half of the looms in the country were located within a hundred-mile radius of Charlotte.

The textile industry did not build cities, however, to the extent that other industries did in other parts of the country during the late nineteenth century. This development reflected the dominance of rural culture in the South. Tompkins and his colleagues rarely located their mills in the midst of existing cities; the factories were either built on the outskirts of those cities or set away in mill villages specifically designed for the purpose. The influences of urban life, it was felt, would prove distracting to the mill operatives, or "lintheads" as townspeople derisively referred to them. Also, because mill owners drew their work force from surrounding farms, the urban periphery or the mill village was better situated to take advantage of this ready supply of labor. Mill workers often brought with them to the mill village their kin, their religious practices, their gardens, and even their farm animals, thereby re-creating as closely as possible the rural life they had left behind. And sometimes they did not even leave that life behind. Although most Americans associate commuting with the white-collar suburbanite, mill workers were the archetypal commuters of an earlier era, though they rarely dashed at today's hectic pace. They either made daily trips to the mill (made easier once the automobile came into general use by the 1920s) or moved back and forth from farm to mill at periodic intervals.

In the meantime, the larger cities of the Piedmont, such as Greensboro and Charlotte, housed the administrative and banking functions that supported the mills and the railroads, as well as the residences of such textile-mill magnates as D. A. Tompkins in Charlotte and Moses and Ceasar Cone in Greensboro. But in the communities that actually hosted the mills, life revolved around the mill and little else. Mill owners either owned the town or developed cozy relationships with community leaders and law enforcement agencies. They succeeded in keeping out both unions and competing industries. The wages they paid limited the buying power of their work force and hence the urban economy as well. Gaston County, North Carolina, located next door to Charlotte, had more textile mills than any other county in the United States in 1920, yet the U.S. Bureau of the Census still classified it as a rural county.

Reforming and Re-creating the Middle Landscape

The textile industry added a new tier to the class hierarchy of the urban South. Some mill towns had separate shopping days for "lintheads," blacks, and everyone else, respectively. Members of the rising urban middle class, self-conscious of their newness and desirous of attaining a legitimacy in the eyes of the ruling elite, were particularly condescending toward mill operatives. Child-labor reforms, compulsory education, temperance movements, health services, and local government reform were urban middle-class good works that placed the South in the mainstream of Progressive sentiment at the turn of the century. But they also revealed an attempt to sanitize and acculturate what writer and planter William Alexander Percy called "a lower form of Anglo-Saxon."

The rise of the urban middle class in these budding Piedmont metropolises was, in the long run, at least as momentous as the growth of the textile industry. Despite the racial and class bias pervading its reform efforts, this class accomplished an impressive array of projects during the late nineteenth and early twentieth centuries. Women in particular took the lead in several areas of reform. The permitted sphere of women's activities was relatively narrow in the Victorian South. But using church organizations (especially in the Methodist denomination) as a base, women's groups effectively lobbied for improvement in education and City Beautiful projects. Their justification for such involvement was that the school and the city were natural extensions of the home; just as a good home environment would go a long way toward molding a good person, a well-appointed school and a clean, neatly planned city would accomplish the same goal on a larger, societal scale. So they pushed for parks, statuary, paved roads, broad boulevards, neighborhood landscaping, and, eventually, comprehensive city planning. In 1912 Daisy Denson and her Woman's Club of Raleigh, North Carolina, went so far as to hire the City Beautiful movement's leading spokesman, Charles Mulford Robinson, to prepare a city plan.

Women were not the only urban residents desirous of reforming their environment. Most urban Southerners continued to perceive their cities through the lens of the countryside. Unlike the cities of the North and Midwest, Southern cities were home-grown. Anyone traveling from the countryside to a Southern city in 1900 would not have encountered the marked contrast in environment that would have been notable in journeying from downstate Illinois to Chicago at that same time. In the early years of this century, Southerners attempted to maintain that identification between city and country as closely as possible.

This mentality was especially evident in the rapidity with which urban Southerners launched planned suburban communities. As cities like Atlanta, Charlotte, and Nashville grew after the Civil War, their modest business sections expanded as well. By the 1890s, retail establishments, office buildings, and banks were crowding out residential districts in the downtown areas. The increased noise and air pollution and the disappearance of open spaces jarred the sensitivities of urban dwellers. Those who could afford to do so moved outward to new residential areas built on former cotton patches and other agricultural land. Such entrepreneurs as Charlotte's Edward Dilworth Latta and Atlanta's Joel Hurt hired nationally known landscape architects and planners, including the Olmsted brothers and John C. Nolen, to design their suburban developments. In addition, these entrepreneurs provided access to and from the downtown by means of their electric trolley lines.

For all their reputed backwardness, urban leaders in the South were eager to try new-fangled inventions, if for no other reason than to get a jump on rival cities and to appear "progressive" to outside investors. Engineer and inventor Frank Sprague took his electric trolley design to several Northern cities, including New York, but was rebuffed. His proposal seemed too fanciful. Besides, some feared that when the electric current passed from the overhead wires down through the trolley, the passengers would be electrocuted—a prospect unlikely to build support for public transit. Sprague found a more receptive audience in the South. (Perhaps life was cheaper there; or, more likely, the design appealed to the booster mentalities of urban leaders.) In 1888 Richmond, Virginia, became the first city in the nation to install an electric trolley system, followed shortly by Montgomery, Alabama. By the 1890s, the trolley was becoming the major facilitator for suburban development. Streetcar suburbs such as Dilworth and Myers Park in Charlotte and Druid Hills in Atlanta provided commodious retreats from the congestion of urban life for upper- and middle-class families.

Some urban residents could not escape, of course, especially blacks. As cities grew, so did the practice of segregation. Separation of the races had existed in the Old South, but it was not codified. The vast majority of blacks had resided as slaves on plantations, where segregation was not an issue. In the cities, blacks and whites mingled occasionally. Segregation as a system appeared during the Reconstruction era, when, ironically, blacks and their Republican allies promoted it as a way for blacks to participate in aspects of urban life from which they previously had been excluded. Schools, public conveyances, and theaters became open to blacks, albeit on a segregated basis. When it became apparent that segregated facilities also meant inferior ones, blacks protested, but to no avail. By the 1890s, segregation was not only the custom in many Southern cities, it was also the law.

Southern urban blacks lived in a twilight zone during this period. Though there were no ghettos comparable to the ones forming in New York's Harlem and Chicago's South Side, residential segregation tightened. Black city dwellers generally lived in low-lying areas or on the urban periphery beyond the range of building codes. Visitors detected these areas easily: the streets were usually unpaved and basic urban services such as trash collection and water and sewer hookups were absent or sporadic even as late as the 1950s. The housing was primarily an urban adaptation of the rural shotgun shack, so named because one could open the front door, fire a gun, and the pellets would exit through the rear door; all the rooms opened off this long, narrow corridor. The shacks were usually constructed of wood, with tar-paper roofs, newspaper for insulation, and, occasionally, a window.

A visit to a black urban school confirmed the inequality of segregation, if further evidence were necessary. These schools were equipped with second-hand or thirdhand textbooks, or no textbooks at all, and most teachers had little more than an eighth-grade education; children of varying ages crowded into classrooms and hallways, sometimes one hundred to a room; and the curriculum stressed vocational subjects and ensured humility and "good citizenship." The urban South and its economic accompaniments after 1900 might very well have represented an advance for the region as a whole. But for blacks, cities merely reflected the same character of race relations pioneered on the plantations. Slavery had stamped blacks as inferior in the Old South; segregation performed the same role in the New South.

False Profits

Blacks, as a part of Southern urban life, were largely invisible to whites. Urban leaders primarily were devoted, as ever, to pursuing the brass ring of economic growth, trying to out-Yankee the Yankee. That objective consumed their endeavors. By the 1920s, many Southern cities had streamlined their political apparatus through the city manager or commission form of government—innovations that, like the electric trolley, debuted in the South. The objective behind both systems was to make government more businesslike, that is, distance it as far as possible from electoral politics. Southern leaders historically were suspicious of democracy, and the Populist movement of the 1890s confirmed their worst fears about universal suffrage. They engineered new voting and registration procedures that severely limited black suffrage and restricted the access of poor whites to the ballot box. These movements had their urban counterparts in the city manager and the administrative commission. Both state and city leaders passed off their new procedures under the guise of reform.

Once urban leaders had arranged their political systems in businesslike modes, they launched a crusade for economic development. The New South Creed had been around for nearly half a century by the 1920s, but the ascendancy of younger, more aggressive middle-class leaders in the interior cities, coupled with the national prosperity and good feeling that followed World War I, triggered an orgy of boosterism. Sinclair Lewis's Zenith may have provided the metaphor for the untrammeled boosterism of the Midwest, but numerous communities in the South could rival that fictional metropolis. During the twenties, Northern and foreign entrepreneurs began to take over the largely indigenous Southern textile industry. Cities embarked on major building projects, heedlessly destroying historic districts and buildings and erecting skyscrapers. Journalist W. J. Cash quipped that Southern cities had as much need for these skyscrapers as "a hog has for a mourning coat." Thomas Wolfe complained about his native Asheville, North Carolina: "A spirit of drunken waste and wild destructiveness was everywhere apparent. The fairest places in the town were being mutilated at untold cost." This was the beginning of a long journey across the river of forgetfulness for many Southern cities, as if the building orgies would somehow wipe away the pain of sectional inferiority, regional poverty, and dependence. Their rural heritage was thrust aside; only sloth and snobbery saved others like New Orleans and Charleston.

It is not surprising that, at this time, a fundamentalist revival swept the South, capturing both urban and rural areas across the region. Poor country folk had come to town, had sinned in excess, and now were ready for redemption. Evangelists prayed for their souls and begged for their money. They succeeded in convincing redeemed politicians to pass a string of blue laws in Southern cities to protect the sanctity of the Sabbath.

Eventually there was a divine judgment of sorts, even if it came from New York City: the Great Depression. Economic development had proved as elusive under the new prophets as under the old. Southern cities were ill equipped, with their traditions of low taxes and limited social services, to deal with massive unemployment, migrations to the city caused by the dislocations in agriculture, and the resulting strain on urban infrastructures such as water and sewer systems. Birmingham put its parks on the auction block in a desperate attempt to raise funds. New Orleans and Atlanta cut back sharply on city personnel and services in order to save money. Southern cities historically had relied on private, church-related charities to provide poor relief. The extent of unemployment during the depression, however, soon wiped out these resources.

Federal Salvation

Fortunately for Southern cities and for the South, the New Deal rescued their citizens and their services. Between 1933 and 1939, three federal agencies—the Federal Emergency Relief Administration (FERA), the Public Works Administration (PWA), and the Works Progress Administration (WPA)—sent nearly $2 billion to the South, most of it to the region's cities. The grants alleviated unemployment to some extent and altered the urban skyline and infrastructure. Sewers, parks, new or renovated government office buildings, hospitals, bridges, and playgrounds—the types of services and structures that Southern cities had not provided even in good times— now appeared on the urban landscape through federal benevolence. The federal government paid for those capital facilities in Southern cities that Northern cities had bought for themselves in earlier decades, and on which they were still paying off the debts. The almost-free modernization received by Southern cities proved an important economic advantage in subsequent decades. The first down payment on the Sunbelt occurred in the 1930s.

The next installment was paid during World War II, when the federal government sent a whopping $7 billion south in the form of defense contracts and military installations. Some historians claim that the impact of the Second World War on the South was at least as significant as that of the Civil War. There is much to recommend this argument. Federal assistance, especially to Southern urban industry, achieved a pump-priming effect on the urban economy. The government helped to stimulate new industries, as in Houston (petrochemicals), and released old ones from colonial restrictions, as in Birmingham (discriminatory freight rates on steel products). Military spending in Southern cities encouraged the development of electronics research and manufacturing firms, scientific equipment companies, and aeronautics machinery plants. Today, many newcomers in the South have come to work for firms that may very well have benefited directly or indirectly from this federal wartime assistance. The growth of high-technology industry has had a positive impact on a region historically burdened with a low-technology, low-wage rural job market. Between 1940 and 1960, the high-wage industrial sector increased by 180 percent in the South, compared with a national rate of 92 percent. By the later date, low-wage industries accounted for only two out of every five manufacturing jobs in the region.

All That Glitters

Southern cities emerged from the war brimming with federal dollars and optimism. The South in general was feeling confident and prosperous, and, as always, cities took their cues from the region. The first major change that occurred in Southern cities was the transformation of local government. For years in most cities, a tight-knit group of businessmen had controlled political life. They had conducted the city's business informally among themselves, over lunch or on the golf course. Their public lives were extensions of their private affairs. But if cities were to take advantage of new economic opportunities, and if they were going to be able to cope with rapid population growth as the traditional farm economy collapsed, a more structured system was necessary. Younger men—attorneys, real estate developers, and bankers— began pushing the older leadership to expand the circle of power and to initiate creative policies. In Houston, for example, a small group of business leaders convened periodically in Room 8F of the Lamar Hotel to socialize and devise policy. As the city grew rapidly after the war, this type of exclusivity proved inefficient and frustrating. By the mid-1950s, new business leaders emerged and put forward one of their own, Lewis Cutrer, to run against Oscar Holcombe, the candidate of the "8F Crowd." Cutrer won with the help of black votes—another new force in postwar Southern urban politics.

A more inclusive political system clamored for a broader economic base. Industrial recruitment became systematized, with cities and urban counties forming permanent bodies to lobby prospective clients, prepare brochures, and generally promote their respective localities. These were not new tactics, but they were undertaken with a new sophistication. Tax incentives and cheap, nonunion labor were still powerful drawing cards in the South, but quality-of-life issues, the level and frequency of services, and the condition of schools also became important factors in the recruiting equation. This meant that the traditional laid-back attitude of urban government toward services and revenues needed to change. And it did to some degree, though the services remained skewed to the business district and the better neighborhoods, and the tax increases (especially the sales tax) weighed heaviest on the poor. What did not change was the employment of Yankee standards of growth in a Southern setting. And in the accommodating climate of the South, those standards continued to be exaggerated. The inferiority complex persisted.

The Southern urban penchant for the megaproject received a boost from the federal government's urban renewal policies during the 1950s and 1960s. To image-conscious urban leaders, a glittering downtown signaled progress and prosperity. They scarcely considered the social costs of such recasting; they never had before, and the poor, black and white, historically had been weak political constituencies. Inner-city, primarily black neighborhoods fell to the wrecking ball; instead of new housing for the poor, new high-rise office buildings, hotels, and convention centers appeared. Atlanta, typically in the vanguard of these trends, erected a vast hotel, shopping, and restaurant complex known as Peachtree Center. Forming the centerpiece was the Hyatt Regency Hotel, capped on its twenty-first story with a revolving bar. The Hyatt touched off a "can-you-top-this?" wave of hotel building in the city. The Omni Hotel, built on the site of a new indoor sports arena, featured a half-acre ice-skating rink in its lobby. The Peachtree Plaza Hotel emerged as the quintessential monument to downtown kitsch. The seventy-story glass and steel silo (the tallest hotel in the world) rises above the downtown like an upright Tower of Pisa with less than one-tenth the charm. A half-acre lagoon dominates the atriumlike lobby, and, of course, a revolving bar spins tourists and conventioneers happily high above the city. It seems like a giant put-on that has been taken seriously.

Less amusing was the fact that, in Southern cities during this period, for every five residents displaced by such projects officials constructed replacement housing for only one. This compared with a national ratio of three to one. The downtown had been saved, but for whom? As a young Atlantan, poised to leave the Emerald City of the Piedmont for the refuge of a small town outside the metropolitan area, blurted to journalist Marshall Frady: "Hell, you talk about *Gone with the Wind*, Sherman and the Civil War were only an illusion, for all the smoke and roar. This time, without anybody ev noticing it, it's really happening. The South is vanishing quietly as a passin, of summer light—and this time for good."

A Return to Roots

But the urban South was redeemed in spite of itself. In retrospect, the redemption is not surprising. By the 1960s, the Southern city had wandered far from its rural roots; it had exchanged heritage for glitz and scale for size. To some extent, this exaggerated redevelopment was part of Southern culture, too: part of being left behind; part of defeat and poverty and humiliation. Rapid development offered an opportunity to make up for lost time, to demonstrate the Southern city's worthiness to be entered onto the lists of modern metropolises. But Southerners could not run away from their history, and when they stopped trying, they did better things. The turnaround began in the mid-1960s and continued through the 1980s. Once urban leaders found a way to turn their cities' neglected heritage into profit, everyone became a historic preservationist. With the rapid construction of a national interstate highway network, an increase in disposable income, a lengthening of vacation time, and a lower average retirement age, people were on the move—either on vacations or to establish new homes in better climates. New Orleans, Savannah, Charleston, and especially Williamsburg, Virginia, soared high on tourist itineraries.

Preservation was not only for the sake of the tourists. The destructiveness of urban renewal created an instant coalition among blacks and preservationists, who worked for a change at city hall. Fueling this trend was the voracious appetite for territory that Southern cities had demonstrated. Annexation was a relatively easy procedure in the South (unlike elsewhere), and local governments had aggressively pursued a population and economic base that were fleeing to the suburbs. In 1945, for example, Houston comprised a modest 73 square miles. Thirty years later, it had ballooned to 556 square miles, with an option on annexing an additional 2,000 square miles. In fact, were it not for these spectacular suburban accessions, most Southern cities would have lost population during the 1970s. In Georgia, where annexation statutes are among the stiffest in the region, Atlanta has lost population and employment to the surrounding suburbs. Between 1975 and 1985, 80 percent of new jobs in the Atlanta area were located outside the city limits.

But territorial aggrandizement has had its costs. The need and expense of extending services to these far-flung districts restricted services and maintenance in older, inner-city neighborhoods. Groups from these neighborhoods joined the anti–urban renewal constituency to form a powerful political coalition in Southern cities during the 1970s. In addition, the 1965 Voting Rights Act gave a strong boost to black voter registration and participation as well as to district representation. The result was a political revolution at the local level even more extensive than the changes in the political process that had immediately followed the Second World War. The new preservation–minority neighborhood coalition—memberships in the two groups overlapped—succeeded in electing governments in New Orleans, Atlanta, Charlotte, Houston, and Richmond. At the same time, the federal government embarked on a reassessment of its misguided urban renewal policies, and in 1974, the Community Development Act began channeling funds to urban neighborhoods to preserve rather than destroy historic buildings.

This does not mean that Southern cities came to have a fly-in-amber quality about them, or that they attempted to make a career out of genteel decay. Preservation has been both a creative strategy and an important link with the past in a region where the past is important for its own sake. True, graceful old neighborhoods such as the Fan District in Richmond and Myers Park in Charlotte are strictly for the affluent. But such neighborhoods as Dilworth in Charlotte and Ansley Park in Atlanta are decidedly middle class. And in Charleston, Mayor Joe Riley has adapted the famed Charleston single house as a prototype for public housing.

In downtown districts, the watchword is "human scale." Numerous cities are returning to their original downtown sites and re-creating the activities that flourished during an earlier era (usually during the late nineteenth century). Some of the more successful adaptations include the Shockoe Slip area of Richmond and Front Street in Savannah. Though the shops are now called "boutiques" (and therefore charge 25 percent more than comparable stores), and though the historic re-creations are often fanciful rather than factual, the point is that history has become a major strategy for the downtown South. There have also been serious attempts to include a residential component in the new-old downtowns; many such residential districts were neglected or demolished in the aggressive postwar era. Charlotte's Fourth Ward, an erstwhile middle-income residential community in the downtown area, was a series of overgrown, empty lots strewn with refuse and dotted with an occasional dilapidated structure. In 1976, through the vision of entrepreneur Dennis Rash and the NCNB (North Carolina National Bank) Community Development Corporation, in cooperation with the city and federal governments, existing structures were saved and others were trucked into the area from elsewhere in the city. Through judicious infill (construction of architecturally compatible dwellings), the developers re-created a late-nineteenth-century urban neighborhood that became a favorite location for so-called yuppies in the early 1980s.

Yuppies have not been the only beneficiaries of the urban renaissance. Just south of Savannah's revitalizing downtown stands a forty-five-block neighborhood known as the Victorian District, replete with distinctive woodframe, gingerbread-style houses erected between 1870 and 1900. Once a fashionable area, the district had fallen into disrepair by the early 1970s, the homes subdivided into rental properties. It seemed likely, though, that the rehabilitation fever in the city would eventually affect even this neighborhood. The residents, predominantly poor, black, elderly renters, would be unable to survive the speculative mania that would descend on the area. In 1977 investment banker Leopold Adler II brought together an interracial group of neighborhood leaders, bankers, architects, and preservation specialists to form a nonprofit development corporation, the Savannah Landmark Rehabilitation Project. The objective was to renovate roughly one-third of the eight-hundred-odd homes in the district without displacing their low-income residents. Financed initially by federal subsidies and then by private syndicates wishing to take advantage of historic-structure tax benefits, Savannah Landmark attained its goal in 1984.

The Suburban City

Renewed interest in the downtown as a retail center, marketplace, and residence formed an interesting counterpoint to peripheral development. By the 1970s, some of the South's suburban cities had begun to grow together like giant underground platelets. Geographers call these growth patterns conurbations, a formless urban mass. If a picture of oozing settlement comes to mind, that is an accurate depiction. A comparable but different settlement pattern would be the Boston–Washington, D.C., corridor or "megalopolis." Cities along a two-hundred-mile corridor of I-85 from Raleigh, North Carolina, to Greenville, South Carolina, are slowly growing together to form a giant conurbated chain that will eventually link up with Richmond on the northern end of the interstate and with Atlanta at its southern tip. The interstate highway (like the earlier Southern Railway) forms a vital transportation bond, and several of the cities within this Piedmont conurbation share regional airports, further blurring urban boundaries. A newer conurbation is emerging along the Gulf Coast, expanding from Pensacola, Florida, to New Orleans and encompassing federal installations and growing port facilities as well as rapidly developing tourist and retirement communities.

These new types of urban settlements sprouting along the Southern landscape have confounded urbanists more accustomed to Northern models of city growth. Brian J. L. Berry, a geographer, termed the pattern "urbanization without cities," and Pat Watters of the Southern Regional Council declared that the South "had no real cities," even referring to Atlanta as "an overgrown county seat." But if Southern cities have not conformed to traditional perspectives on urbanization, they may herald a new era in American urbanization. In other words, rather than being urban mutations, these sprawling low- and medium-density creations may be the forerunners of a new urban America—one more dependent on the automobile, with a dispersed population and economic base, in proximity to the countryside and recreational amenities, and with predominantly low-rise residential and commercial structures. It is a more private, less confrontational, and more relaxed way of living than the older pattern of urbanization offered. It is Southern.

But the new urban form does not imply immunity from old urban problems. Dependence on the automobile can lead to gridlock. The community focal point is no longer the church, the town hall, or the courthouse, but the highway. Arlington, Texas, midway between the Dallas–Ft. Worth metroplex, is, according to urbanist Paul Geisel, "three highways in search of a city." Its downtown is a jumble of gas stations, fast-food emporiums, and car dealerships. Civic consciousness is nonexistent: the average turnout for municipal elections is 10 percent of the eligible electorate. The "older" neighborhoods, erected in the 1950s, are going to seed, and traffic jams mar access to declining commercial strips. In a generation, Arlington has gone from nothing to nowhere.

Even for older, more established cities, there are potential headaches that sound very familiar to refugees from the erstwhile promised land of the North: the retreat of population and economic base beyond where annexation can grab them; crime rates in Atlanta, Miami, and Dallas that rival the supposed crime capitals of the North; a broad gap, as cities become more sprawling, between the location of the unemployed (the inner city) and the location of jobs (usually on the periphery) that can utilize the low skill levels of these individuals; the environmental costs of development, especially for expanding resort communities in sensitive coastal areas; and the renewed vigor of once-prostrate cities in the Midwest and Northeast that are now better able to compete for investment dollars. Houston has become the epitome of what could happen: all-day rush hours; frequent breaks in overtaxed water lines; an overextended police force, requiring merchants and some wealthy residents to employ their own private guards; overpumping of underground aquifers, causing the gradual sinking of the city; the increased possibility of flooding; and, in November 1983, in obvious biblical judgment, a plague of locusts. Perhaps the past is catching up to the future.

Country Cosmopolites

But the Houston scenario, nightmarish as it is, is unlikely to herald the future of the urban South. Southern cities have become, for better or worse, the main repositories of regional culture. With the demographic and economic decline of the countryside and of small towns after World War II, the future of the region came to reside in the cities. But instead of setting new cultural directions, Southern urbanites, usually with newcomers as their willing ac-. complices, have maintained and refined the older culture. Church barbecues, neighborhood festivals, home tours, and concerts and craft fairs in the park remain the most common embodiments of culture and entertainment in today's Southern city. These events reflect a small-town heritage and the desire to keep it that way. The small town (fewer than 10,000 residents), in fact, remains the most characteristic Southern urban settlement today. It is a cultural prototype as well.

Planners are continually preaching "small is beautiful." Northern cities happened on the concept in the 1970s because that was all they could afford; Southern cities embraced it because it was their culture. Things are apt to move at a slower pace in the urban South, and manners and etiquette are not endangered species. In Southern cities one can hear the native music—jazz, bluegrass, country, and rhythm and blues—and eat the indigenous food. A visit to the Rendezvous in Memphis for some ribs, or Ted's in Birmingham and Gus's in Charlotte for some fried okra and pecan pie (both restaurants are owned by good ol' Greeks), or the Elite (pronounced EE-light) Cafe in Montgomery for fried chicken, or most anywhere in New Orleans for whatever's on the menu will provide a taste of the South.

The urban South began in the forest and, in some respects, never left it, though from time to time, in a welter of shrill boosterism, its cities have lost their way. The fact that cities in today's South are becoming more cosmopolitan is not proof positive of a cultural lobotomy. As Southern poet and literary critic Allen Tate put it: "Provincialism is that state of mind in which . . . men lose their origin in the past and its continuity into the present, and begin every day as if there had been no yesterday." The stock "good ol' boy" is not representative of the South. This Southern type, Paul Hemphill noted, is "out in the suburbs now, living in identical houses and shopping at the K-Mart and listening to Glen Campbell (Roy Acuff and Ernest Tubb are too tacky now) and hiding their racism behind code words. They have forfeited their style and spirit, traded it all in on a color TV and styrofoam beams for the den."

The insights of Tate and Hemphill are supported by the research of John Shelton Reed. He has found that cosmopolitan Southerners serve to strengthen rather than to obliterate regional distinctions, especially since the Southern way of life has come to correspond with our changing concept of the "good life." The South is still fresh and exciting—not necessarily with the heedless pioneer mentality of yore, though traces of that attitude combine with a new self-congratulatory tone about regional progress. Rather, its excitement comes from a society that still adheres to traditions now moribund in most other places yet uses that culture to forge a better civilization in the modern world. The frontier for fulfilling that experiment is the Southern metropolis. And the fulfillment depends, in part, on the contributions and understanding of people who have come from other regions and nations to live in the New South.

Ladies, Belles, Working Women, and Civil Rights

JULIA KIRK BLACKWELDER

Since 1964 I have lived in the South as a non-Southerner. In that year I left my hometown in upstate New York and settled in Atlanta, Georgia. I was almost twenty-one years old, I had recently graduated from the University of Pennsylvania, and I had just married a Southern Gentleman. In the 1960s the South blazed with the passion of the civil rights movement. White Southerners buzzed about the indignities committed by "uppity Negras." During my first summer in Atlanta, civil rights activists pressed their campaigns to desegregate the city's public accommodations. Middle-class citizens on Atlanta's lily-white Northside circulated the rumor that blacks integrating Leb's, a popular downtown delicatessen, had urinated on the dining tables. At Hartsfield Airport, the managers of the food concessions installed their version of the Berlin Wall: a partition that would allow blacks to be served in the airport restaurant without breaking white habits of racial segregation.

When Viola Liuzzo was shot in Alabama in March 1965, a neighbor lady told me the "truths" about Liuzzo that had not been reported in the newspaper. The national press had carried the story of the violent death of a middle-aged white housewife from Michigan who had ferried supplies for the Selma-to-Montgomery marchers. But my neighbor confided that her brother was a deputy sheriff in Alabama and had been at the civil rights march during which Liuzzo was killed. Through him, she had heard that Liuzzo had a black boyfriend and that she had puncture marks from hypodermic needles all over her arms and legs.

In the South, race and gender have twisted together like vines of wisteria, ensuring that the rights of Southern blacks could not be advanced entirely in isolation from the rights of women. Nineteenth-century diarist Fanny Kemble Knight, the wife of a South Carolina plantation owner, understood that the oppression of black men and women under slavery also compromised white women. Today, in the South, black men who disparage women or white women who disparage blacks also inadvertently disparage themselves. At the height of the Black Power movement, Stokely Carmichael was asked what position women had in the movement. Carmichael reportedly answered that the only position for women was "on their backs." Stokely Carmichael was not a thoughtful rights advocate, and he also was not a Southerner.

In the atmosphere of the 1960s, Yankee women who had attended "liberal" Ivy League institutions were definitely suspect in the South. In the early years of my life as the wife of a Southern Gentleman, I tried to act like the cautious outsider I clearly was. The trouble was my tongue. It kept jumping around inside my mouth; even when I bit it, "white liberal" words would come tumbling out. Whether it was youthful self-righteousness or the anguish of the times, I found it hard to live in the South of the 1960s.

Both for me and for the South that has become my home, much has changed since the 1960s, but some habits of mind have persisted. The black and white university students whom I now teach have never heard of Viola Liuzzo or Stokely Carmichael, and they never knew segregation. Blacks and women now compete with white males, often successfully, for jobs formerly denied them.

During the 1970s, urban renewal projects destroyed the most visible evidence of an older South, the South of black shanties and dilapidated white mill villages. Bulldozers leveled most of these and replaced them with highways and public housing projects. At the fringes of most Southern cities, however, remnants of the South of the 1950s still stand. Some old mill

houses and tenant shacks seem to have stood by faith alone since their creation in the late nineteenth or early twentieth century.

In major Southern cities today, visitors note the many well-dressed, immaculately groomed black and white professional women and housewives whom they see in offices, on the streets, and in suburban shopping centers. These are the Southern ladies of the 1980s and 1990s, but they are mostly self-made ladies. Few can claim "Southern ladies" or "Southern belles"—in the antebellum sense—as their ancestors, although their mothers and grandmothers may well have been ladylike. The average middle-class Southerner, black or white, has not been separated from the humble environment of small farms and mill villages by more than a generation or two. Prosperity is a new idea in the South.

The "belle" and the "lady" are the two traditional models of feminine behavior in the South. Both presuppose a rigidly patriarchal society and sufficient material well-being to permit "refined" behavior. Patriarchy has a long history in the South, but until very recently, relatively few families have enjoyed material well-being. Consequently, there has always been tension between the ideals of female behavior and the reality of most women's lives.

Feminism, as opposed to femininity, has no place in the norms of Southern society, although some Southern women have chosen to reject these norms.

Images of acceptable female behavior have supposedly descended from the era of the Lost Cause, but they are actually rooted in the creations of late-nineteenth- and early twentieth-century culture, including Margaret Mitchell's *Gone with the Wind*, the United Daughters of the Confederacy, and fundamentalist religion. In the antebellum period, ideals of feminine behavior did not differ greatly between the North and the South. The religious revivalism of the 1820s and 1830s stressed the mission of women as homemakers and mothers. The ideal mother was a model of patience and Christian virtue whose capacity for nurture could ensure the moral righteousness of her children. Nevertheless, women were believed to be physically and intellectually inferior to men and therefore rightly guided by them. Rigorous schooling and advanced education or constant exposure to business or politics would, it was thought, lead to a woman's emotional and physical collapse. Strenuous physical activity endangered women's capacity to bear healthy children.

Although there have always been differences between women's roles in the North and in the South, sectional differences in gender ideals diverged further in the late nineteenth century. In the North, educators and writers like Catharine Beecher and her more famous sister, Harriet Beecher Stowe, began to preach that rigorous physical exercise and extended schooling strengthened rather than weakened women for their roles as wives and mothers. The founders of the Seven Sisters colleges believed that educated women were capable of higher moral judgment than women of little education. When the first generation of women graduated from Northern colleges around the turn of the century, some of them sought careers. Women like Jane Addams preserved the feminine ideal of moral nurture, but they extended that role beyond the home. A few women, again like Addams, even entered the sphere of politics. Jane Addams herself was driven to her work by a moral fervor imbued by her Protestant upbringing. Girls growing up in the South in the late nineteenth century knew this same Protestant commitment to good works, but the limits of women's expectations and the assumptions underlying good works were very different in the South.

In the South after the Civil War, gender roles developed along lines compatible with a society that was largely rural, overwhelmingly Protestant, racially segregated, and distinguished by poverty. In the struggle of white Southern men to define a world without slavery and to reclaim politics and business from the carpetbaggers, gender took on a meaning and a political importance it held nowhere else in America. The lady of the plantation became a symbol of lost virtue. Having failed to keep her safe during the war, gentlemen subsequently were obliged to protect her against ravishment by the conquerors. Sherman had raped the land, but the same fate would not befall Southern women.

The investment of the Southern lady as a symbol of the Lost Cause bore heavily on the real prospects of all Southern women. According to this new view, moral purity was the central tenet of womanhood, and all else descended from it. Ladies should be refined and passionless. A lady would never kiss a man who had not publicly announced his intent to marry her. Sexual intercourse was not pleasurable, but rather a wifely obligation for which childbirth and motherhood were sacred rewards. Unlike the older American model of the Christian mother, the Southern lady's role was to be rather than to do. A wife's vocation was to enhance the comfort, social status, and masculinity of her husband, and courtship revolved around the woman's need to demonstrate that she could fulfill these roles. Beauty, grace, "breeding," deference, and flattery were all indications of a girl's suitability for marriage. A man hoping to capture the girl of his dreams likewise engaged in flattery, but not in deference. The better equipped the suitor was to offer material comfort and social standing, the more his attentions were encouraged by a prospective bride and her family.

In the context of Protestant religion, the Southern lady's moral fervor propelled her in the direction of moral perfectionism. Virtue, it was thought, could be achieved by isolating oneself from worldly sins and consequently from the world itself. Education beyond bare literacy and basic feminine refinements was believed dangerous. Although charity and proselytization were basic to both Southern and Northern evangelicalism, they manifested themselves in ways that suited each individual culture. As part of their Christian duties, Southern ladies organized and participated in institutions for aiding the orphaned, the infirm, and the elderly. Churchwomen supported missionary activities throughout the world, and an occasional Southern lady took up the missionary life, but their predominant message was always one of personal salvation, not social or political change.

In the early twentieth century, the image of the belle began to rival that of the lady as a female role model. In *Gone with the Wind*, Margaret Mitchell dramatized both of these types and the tension between them. The belle, Scarlett O'Hara, loses her heartthrob, Ashley Wilkes, to Melanie Hamilton, a true Southern lady. Scarlett's jealousy nearly destroys her, but for all her envy she comes to admire Melanie's virtues. As a Southern lady, Melanie is polite to everyone but defers only to men who are her social equals or betters. Always loving and never discouraged, always charitable and never vindictive, gentle in all her ways but strong enough to kill in defense of her family, Melanie Wilkes finds that her nobility, although tested at every turn, never fails her. The Yankees may destroy Melanie's claims to aristocratic privilege, but they cannot shake her aristocratic character. The ideal Southern woman commands the admiration and devotion of all around her but remains humble and unaffected.

While Mitchell's Melanie Wilkes is the archetypal lady, Scarlett O'Hara is the quintessential belle. A young woman of considerable charm, grace, and beauty, she advances her interests by manipulating other people. Although clever, she never allows men to glimpse her keen intelligence. A belle may evolve into a lady if she abandons her manipulative impulses as she matures, but Scarlett O'Hara is unable to overcome her desire to dominate and control others. At the end of the novel she stands protected by her accumulated wealth but stripped of love and respect.

Scarlett O'Hara and Melanie Wilkes have no more grounding in history than Twain's celebrated jumping frog of Calaveras County. That is the appeal of Margaret Mitchell's women. They are the larger-than-life characters of Southern tall tales. The immense popularity of *Gone with the Wind* (outsold only by the Bible, as the book's own myth goes) demonstrates the enduring appeal of idealized Southern womanhood. The myth of the belle and the lady hatched and grew on Southern soil, but the romantic instincts of readers throughout America and the rest of the world have kept the myth alive.

In the mythical antebellum South depicted in literature, the violently patriarchal relationships between white men and everyone around them become the dominant force in the economic and political culture of the region. The writings of William Faulkner, Robert Penn Warren, and other Southern literary giants convey the idea that the violent legacies of slavery and chivalric sexual oppression have poisoned the world of twentieth-century Southerners as well. Although most of these works are fictional, they articulate accurately the assumptions of many twentieth-century Southerners. Even in those literary offerings in which race does not play a direct role, we frequently confront white female characters whose lives are bounded by notions drawn from a selectively remembered plantation past. In Tennessee Williams's play *A Streetcar Named Desire*, Blanche DuBois's collapse results from her inability to reconcile her economic circumstances, her marriage to a homosexual man, and her own sexual proclivities with the image of the plantation wife she had hoped to become. Much of the serious Southern fiction of the twentieth century has dramatized the high costs of allegiance to the myths of Southern history.

Unlike the fictional Blanche, twentieth-century Southern women rarely aspire to become the lady of a plantation. Prosperous Southern plantations have simply been too few and far between for most Southerners to have any expectations of such a lifestyle. Nevertheless, the image of the plantation and the concrete example of tumbledown plantation houses that serve as reminders of the Lost Cause have had a real influence on girls growing up in the South. Although few Southern girls dare hope to become a plantation mistress, the notion of the aristocratic Southern lady has been a standard against which they measure themselves. In such a comparison, of course, only the most confident and self-possessed girl will not find herself lacking.

Patriarchal gender and race relationships are central to contemporary Southerners' notions of the Old South, just as they are the heart of twentieth-century Southern literature. The plantation economy created a world in which white men ruled over white women, black men, and black women, but black men did not rule over black women. In this situation, a friendly greeting from a black man to a white woman might constitute sexual assault, but the rape or beating of a black woman by a white man could be considered sport.

Gender roles in the Old South were narrowly circumscribed, but behavioral expectations were not the same for all women. The enormous contrast between the duties and expected behaviors of black and white women is self-evident in the fact of slavery, but there also were significant differences among black women that reflected the jobs assigned by the master or overseer, the religious beliefs of slaves, and the talents or skills of individual women. Free black women could and usually did play to a very different set of expectations than slave women. Among white women in the antebellum South, roles and social constraints derived largely from one's class and religion. Few white women were plantation mistresses, and therefore few were constrained by the veneer of gentility that supposedly marked the Southern lady.

In the early 1970s, historian Ann Firor Scott demonstrated the falseness of the myth of the Southern lady. Plantation mistresses of the antebellum South, she noted, may have been well mannered, well groomed, and socially accomplished, but few lived in luxury. Even fewer plantation mistresses enjoyed leisurely lives free of worldly duties. Most of them bore heavy responsibilities: managing the home and household servants, overseeing the physical care of the slaves, and supervising the production and possible sale of garden crops. Scarlett O'Hara and Melanie Wilkes were invented in the 1920s by an urban journalist seeking to placate the romantic fantasies of women like herself who struggled to find comfort and meaning in difficult personal circumstances. Margaret Mitchell's young adult years were shadowed by a decline in her family's financial well-being and by a disastrous marriage. She worked to support herself and to protect her family from disgrace—a life with striking analogies to the early years of Scarlett O'Hara.

Despite the persistence of a feminine ideal that dictates that women should remain in the home, Southern women throughout the twentieth century have been more likely to seek outside employment than their counterparts in other regions. Some, but not all, of this difference between Southern and non-Southern women is accounted for by the fact that black women in American society have traditionally been workers, and the black population remained concentrated in the South for most of the century. In the early twentieth century most black women engaged in farm labor, but by 1920 domestic work had become their major employment. Black women found few nonagricultural jobs other than as maids, laundresses, charwomen, and untrained nurses. Paid work in the domestic sphere lured black women into villages, towns, and cities and consequently altered the lifestyles of black families. However, black women remained at the lower end of the wage scale. The average urban or rural black family with one or two working adults found itself at the bottom of the income ladder.

Historically, the greatest differences among Southern women have been those of race. The legacy of slavery is a historical reminder of the magnitude of differences between black and white women, but twentieth-century disparities are the consequences of racial discrimination in a free society. The most obvious and most easily documented differences between blacks and whites in America have been economic ones. As a group, black Americans are poorer than whites and always have been, although the economic gap has fluctuated over time. Poverty has required most black women to work for wages throughout most of their adult lives and often during childhood as well. Working mothers are now a fact of life among all ethnic and racial groups in America, but for black Americans they are a historical as well as a contemporary phenomenon.

Poverty explains partly but not wholly why black wives have been more likely to work than have white wives. Particular groups of immigrants—Mexican Americans of the 1920s, for example—have also been very poor but have seldom sent married women out to work. One factor that has encouraged black mothers to stay in the labor force has been their greater likelihood of being household heads because of separation, divorce, widowhood, or other circumstances. However, black wives whose spouses are still in the household have also been more likely to work than have other wives. Unlike many immigrant groups, blacks have a historical tradition of wifely employment, and black wives who wish to work have not faced the same level of familial or communal criticism that Italian or Mexican wives have. Over time black Americans have also built up stronger child-care networks among their kin to accommodate the mothers' working.

Southern white women have also been more likely to work for wages or otherwise contribute to the family's earnings than have white women elsewhere in the United States. The high work rate among all women is a principal reason why the myth of the Southern lady so sharply contrasted with the experience of most Southern women, white and black. In an agricultural economy, women and men, girls and boys went into the fields to help the tenant family make its crops. Black wives and white wives supplemented the family's income from cotton or tobacco by raising food products for family consumption and frequently for sale as well.

Both racial segregation and the overwhelming poverty of Southerners were inducements for manufacturers to develop textile, fibers, and tobacco factories in the South before World War II. All of these industries relied heavily on the labor of women. Until World War II, boys and girls commonly began factory work before reaching their sixteenth birthdays, and workers under the age of eighteen can still be found in such industries today. The appearance of factories provided women with a greater opportunity to help support their families than had their farm labor. In the short run, those families who could keep mothers, sons, and daughters employed were better off than struggling farm tenants, who faced the vagaries of weather, blight, and uncertain prices. In the long run, however, the factories stamped a legacy of doom on families who gave up all of their members to the work force. Schools began to train children primarily for factory or textile mill labor, and secondary schooling was discouraged in mill towns. Children were encouraged to marry at very young ages because it was difficult for an individual to survive outside a family work unit, and because high fertility replenished the factory work forces.

The broad availability of low-wage black domestic workers up until the 1950s meant that the average white homemaker or the white working wife could employ at least one servant. One aspect of the lifestyle of a lady—freedom from domestic drudgery—was within the reach of most white women. Because most middle-class wives and even some working-class wives in the South had domestic help, standards for white homemakers were somewhat higher than they might have been. With assistance in doing their housework, middle-class wives could maintain levels of order that otherwise would have been impossible. Rather than producing a life of leisure for middle-class wives, the presence of servants increased expectations that the "lady" of the house would keep an immaculate home and entertain graciously. Legendary Southern hospitality depended upon a social system in which the lot of some was to further the comfort of others. Such was the task of the white home-maker and the domestic worker who assisted her.

Both the civil rights movement and the Sunbelt economic revolution turned the world of middle-class wives upside down. Beginning in the 1960s, black women rapidly left domestic work for better jobs elsewhere. More and more middle-class white women deserted homemaking for the office. The domestic sphere and the world of female friendships that had marked the day-to-day experience of most white wives in the 1940s had almost disappeared within a twenty-year period.

Even as more and more white women marched off to sales, clerical, and professional jobs, a significant minority of Southern white and middle-class black women took pride in their decisions to make homemaking a full-time career. The choice of home over the workplace is not terribly surprising in a section of the country where the women's liberation movement had less impact than elsewhere, but the strong attachment to the domestic sphere shown by some Southern women of the 1980s is not simply a product of a general Southern social conservatism. If mothers are to remain at home, even temporarily, fathers' income must be high enough to keep families intact. The unprecedented prosperity that has come to the South since World War II has provided some couples with the opportunity to allow wives to remain at home, although their own mothers did not have this choice. Ironically, ordinary white Southern women of the 1960s came closer to the middle-class income level that made it possible for them to remain at home than had any generation before them. Southern black families in the 1950s and 1960s were also more prosperous than at any period before or since.

Yet as general prosperity was pulling some women back to the domestic sphere, the decline in available domestic help was making the work of the housewife more difficult, and the expansion of job opportunities for all women was making the sacrifice of staying at home more costly. Overall, the labor market won out over homemaking. But for those wives, black and white, who remained at home, devotion to child rearing and homemaking was an important symbol of middle-class status in which the whole family could take pride. Southern housewives, regardless of their family income or social class, do not apologize for not being modern superwomen. The evangelical Christianity of the 1970s and 1980s, with its central emphasis on traditional gender roles, has further reinforced a domestic vocation long prescribed but previously unavailable to poor Southern women.

In their expectations and their daily lives, Southern women today are more like their sisters outside the South than they have ever been. Historically, Southern women married younger and bore more children than women elsewhere, but these regional differences have virtually disappeared in the last two decades. Divorce and extramarital fertility have risen in the South as they have nationally. Divorce rates are lower in the Northwest than in the South, but they are higher in the West. Infant mortality rates, once much higher in the South than elsewhere, have now dropped to at or below the national figures. Roughly half of all Southern women are in the labor force, which holds true for women nationally. The numbers of working women in Arkansas, Louisiana, and Mississippi fall considerably below the national rates, but work rates for men in these states are also below the national average.

Southern women today are still noticeably different from other American women, but the differences are mostly matters of custom relating to communication and social interaction. The characteristics that distinguish Southern women from others are the intangible links with an older South. Like the architectural remnants of the past, uniquely Southern behaviors among women are gradually giving way to newer national characteristics as the South moves into the mainstream of the American experience. Nevertheless, girls growing up in Southern families today still inherit and learn traditional gender roles that are rooted in an older society in which both women and blacks held secondary status.

Most American families have traditionally been patriarchal in structure, but in the South patriarchal customs remained strong well into the twentieth century, after they had begun to erode elsewhere. A love of history, allegiance to the past, and the myth of the Southern lady were some reasons that patriarchal values persisted in Southern society. Patriarchy also is linked to the social and economic paternalism that has characterized most of Southern history. How could a man rule a factory or plantation or administer a government for the best interests of the citizenry if he could not rule his own family? In the early twentieth century, employers encouraged their workers to think of the mill "family" or the plantation "family" as a group bound together by mutual interests that went beyond the wage contract. A good employer "took care" of his workers by providing their homes and frequently their stores, churches, and schools as well. In return he felt entitled to loyalty and deference from his employees. In this model of the actual family and the family of capitalist enterprise, there is not much room for uppity workers, uppity children, or uppity women.

The majority of working men in the South found themselves at the wrong end of this paternalistic economic scale. Consequently, such "manly" behaviors as hunting, drinking, fighting, and inflicting absolute authority upon their families were their means of establishing respect in a world in which they were both poor and necessarily loyal to paternalistic bosses. All white men could claim some measure of respect by intimidating or terrorizing black men, but black men had only their wives and children to command. Because they had the lowest earning potential and the fewest opportunities to assume manly or patriarchal roles, black men occupied an unenviable position in a segregated society.

Women's roles within patriarchal families focused around raising children who lived up to fathers' as well as mothers' expectations. Mothers taught children the manners that suited their places in a hierarchical and paternalistic society. Conservative evangelical religion fit hand in glove with patriarchy and paternalism. The new versions of evangelicalism that have proved so attractive to Southern whites in the 1970s and 1980s have reaffirmed the traditional roles of women at a time when economic and social realities have made those roles less tenable than ever before. By contrast, paternalism has declined in the South with the advent of national and international buy-outs. Cotton mills and other industries have sold off their villages, and the overall view of society as patriarchal has faded. Divorce trends and the rising incidence of female-headed households have made the patriarchal family less and less common in the South. In traditional middle-class families, patriar-chy rested partly on the assumption that the husband and father was the family provider, but that situation is increasingly uncommon, and few wives expect *never* to be employed. The reality that a woman can make a measur-able economic contribution to a marriage, even if her husband has superior earnings, works against the concept that husbands should have authority over their wives.

Despite recent changes, the greatest statistical differences between South-ern women and others are in the areas of income and religion. Both the relative poverty of the South and its overwhelming Protestantism continue to affect the ways in which women act. Southern women earn about seventy-five cents for every dollar earned by women outside the South. Nevertheless, the Sunbelt economic boom has reduced unemployment in the South and brought relative prosperity to a region historically shrouded in poverty. Al-though Southern women and Southern families remain poorer than other Americans, income differences between individuals may not be apparent at first meeting. Both the real increase in income and a relative decline in clothing costs have permitted today's poor Southerners to dress better than their ancestors did. Dietary changes, fluoridated water, and improved medi-cal care have given Southerners in general a healthy appearance, although poor Southerners continue to suffer especially high rates of hypertension and heart disease.

Southern women are more likely to be Protestant churchgoers than are women anywhere else in America. In the past, evangelical Protestantism helped Southerners cope with poverty. More recently, the improved earn-ings of Southern families have noticeably changed the lifestyles of women, churchgoing or not. Long the refuge of the dispossessed, the Southern church has had to adjust to the increased prosperity of the Sunbelt. Among women, that adjustment has included a fascination with consumerism earlier condemned by austere fundamentalists.

Before her dethronement in the late 1980s, Tammy Faye Bakker—not a native Southerner—reigned as the queen of Protestant materialism. Al-though their appeal was not strictly regional, Jim and Tammy Faye Bakker were two of the many evangelists of the 1970s and 1980s who popularized the notion that God does not frown on luxurious living by faithful Christians. Such an idea complements the older Southern view that good grooming and a prim but attractive appearance are evidence of proper manners and "good breeding" in a woman. Historically, the feminine ideal in the South revolved around ill-defined and often contradictory images of ladyhood. The one element of the image that has not changed over time is the centrality of good grooming. Tammy Faye Bakker embodied this virtue in her earlier years as the preacher's wife. In her media career, however, Bakker went too far and fell off the pedestal. Her now legendary shopping excesses were not the problem; rather, by appearing in public encrusted in heavy cosmetics and figure-revealing clothing or posing for photographs in skimpy lingerie, Bakker left both good grooming and propriety behind. She became overtly sexy—the provocative Jezebel. And, just as offensive to appropriate female etiquette, she became "tacky."

Neither her overtly sensuous image nor her tackiness, however, caused Tammy Faye Bakker to lose followers. Changing gradually from Southern lady to Jezebel, Bakker came to represent a different but equally strong facet of Southern Protestantism: never having claimed Christian perfectionism, Bakker presented herself before television audiences as the humble sinner whom God mercifully guided down the path toward righteousness. Simultaneously, she projected a carnal image that revealed the lustful nature of sinful males. In the Southern Protestant tradition, God forgives all, but men and women must first come to grips with the sins of the heart (to which Jimmy Carter publicly confessed) and the sins of the flesh (to which the fictional Elmer Gantry capitulated). Twentieth-century Southern preachers have consistently warned their flocks against modern Jezebels, and fundamentalist Southern women have borne the burden of original sin attached to these warnings. Promiscuity is a potential manifestation of original sin among women, and the Southern belle, whose manner is flirtatious, is especially vulnerable. The Southern lady, an essentially passionless person, has successfully overcome the risk of this carnal sin.

Southern religion, although overwhelmingly Protestant and evangelical, has been characterized in the twentieth century by a multiplicity of denominations, sects, cults, and revivalistic movements. Twentieth-century religion also has provided women with many more options than the roles played by Tammy Faye Bakker. In the form of the established black and white denominations that predominated in the nineteenth century, the modern church has been and continues to be a source of moral courage for men and women who have thoughtfully examined Southern society and found its race and class relations to be both un-Christian and unjust. Even though Southern patriarchy discouraged women from participating in campaigns for social justice, the list of women who have been twentieth-century Christian soldiers for social change is a long one. These women have been as poor and socially disadvantaged as Fannie Lou Hamer of the Mississippi Freedom Democratic party of the 1960s or as privileged and "aristocratic" as Lucy Randolph Mason, the great-great-great-granddaughter of the author of the Virginia Declaration of Rights, who was herself a formidable organizer for the Congress of Industrial Organizations (CIO). In the 1920s, a band of women organized through the Young Women's Christian Association (YWCA) led state battles to limit child labor and improve the conditions of women working in Southern mills and factories. Jessie Daniel Ames and Methodist churchwoman Dorothy Rogers Tilley led the fight against lynching in the 1930s.

Episcopalian Lucy Randolph Mason, inspired by her own faith and the tutelage of her clergyman father and activist mother, devoted her life to a variety of efforts that challenged the assumptions of the Virginia aristocracy and refuted the prejudices of most white Southerners. Of her focus on the Southern front, Mason wrote, "When I was fourteen, a missionary's sermon made me want to be a missionary myself. Later, I recognized that religion can be put to work right in one's own community."[1] Mason's commitment led her to prominent roles in the Equal Suffrage League, the League of Women Voters, the YWCA, the National Consumers League, the Union Label League, and the Urban League. The concerns that continuously motivated

---

1. Lucy Randolph Mason, *To Win These Rights: A Personal Story of the CIO in the South* (New York: Harper, 1952), 4.

Mason were social justice and better conditions for industrial workers. Both of these concerns propelled Mason toward the CIO and its organizational drives in the South during the 1930s.

As an organizer, Mason held the upper hand. She rallied workers despite their traditional disdain for female leadership because her ladylike presence in factories was incongruous and because tough-guy union leaders stood by her. Her special gift was gaining a hearing with management and local community leaders. During a strike at Charlotte's Highland Park Mill, Mason expressed surprise at the cordial reception extended to her by J. E. Dowd, managing editor of the *Charlotte News*. Dowd explained that his wife had been in Mason's Sunday school class in Richmond and that her "mild" appearance made her a formidable spokesperson for the union.

The civil rights movement also provided women with role models for active lives outside the home. Rosa Parks, Septima Clark, Anne Moody, and Fannie Lou Hamer have all inspired young Southern women and men. Rosa Parks and Septima Clark stood with Martin Luther King, Jr., and others in organizing desegregation boycotts and marches. Anne Moody joined with other young people in campaigning for desegregation and voter rights in Mississippi. Fannie Lou Hamer led the Mississippi Freedom Democratic party's delegation to the 1968 Democratic National Convention. These women demonstrated a faith as enduring as Mason's, and their strength revealed the extraordinary capacity of many black women to survive segregation and cope with bitter realities but never to capitulate to the injustices regularly visited upon them. Both the historical reliance of black families on the labor of women and a thorough knowledge of white society equipped women like Hamer with the skills and the determination to effect the changes of the civil rights revolution. As Anne Moody revealed in her autobiography, *Coming of Age in Mississippi*, many black girls began their service in white households before they reached their teenage years. As ears in white households, black servants learned both the politics and the secrets of the families who employed them. Such knowledge helped black rights workers plan their strategies and protect themselves from attacks by angry whites.

By the 1980s, many of the promises of Southern social and political activism had dimmed, but the women who participated in these movements left an invaluable legacy to black and white girls in today's South. Instead of the ideals of the belle or the lady, to which few women could ever hope to aspire, the activists of the twentieth century offered Southern women concrete role models. These female leaders presented images that preserved their Southern distinctiveness and at the same time allowed the women to choose goals and lifestyles that complemented rather than denied their family heritages, that confirmed rather than suppressed the development of their individual talents. Such forces as contemporary evangelicalism have attempted to reinstate and reaffirm wholly domestic roles for Southern women, and many women have voluntarily chosen the life of a helpmate for themselves. Some have done so for religious reasons. Others have made the choice because recent prosperity has offered them a release from the exhausting labors pursued by their impoverished mothers and grandmothers. Overall, however, both black and white women in the South continue to enlarge their roles in the economy, society, and politics.

Many women writers in the contemporary South have also confirmed a movement away from the constraining roles of ladies and belles. In her autobiographical *Fatal Flowers*, Rosemary Daniell describes the torture of growing up poor and white among affluent white girls who could afford the refinements of belles and ladies. The material advantages of the middle and upper classes kept poor schoolgirls at a great distance from their more fortunate classmates. Consequently, as a child Daniell had only outward circumstances by which to judge the differences of others. In the shame of her own poverty, she could not really know her affluent classmates but imagined them to lead enchanted and superior lives. Knowing she could never be a "lady," she felt inadequate. During adolescence Daniell also struggled with sexual guilts instilled by her fundamentalist upbringing. In her adult life, however, she was able to chart a new course based on individual accomplishments and free of the constraints of class and gender that had marred her childhood.

In a recent autobiographical essay, contemporary novelist Robb Forman Dew also described the heavy burdens of the ladyhood image. Dew confessed that she abandoned her pretenses to being a Southern belle because "the whole idea of it was so far from the truth, and it required so much energy that I just let all of it drift away."[2] In the novel *Heartbreak Hotel*, Anne Rivers Siddons chronicled a Southern mother's success in marrying her daughter into a "good" family and the subsequent anguish of the daughter who, as a wife and mother, could never measure up to the standards of ladyhood set by her mother-in-law.

Fortunately for the majority of women who will never be Southern belles or Southern ladies—and for the men who will never be plantation gentlemen— the myths of Southern femininity have eroded considerably since World War II. Ironically, it is prosperity that is eating away at the myths. Southerners who are busy getting ahead just do not have time for the sleepy customs associated with the small towns and rural haunts of their parents and grandparents. The "movers and shakers" of the Sunbelt South have found some utility in past behaviors. They have clung to those older manners and behaviors that accommodate the present while jettisoning other behaviors. Whether or not white Southerners are nostalgic for an earlier era, they know that segregation has no more place in the bustling contemporary economy than does dinner at noon. Southern women are no less "Southern" than they ever were, but they have modified their notions of ladyhood. A proper, middle-class matron from the 1920s would shudder to see the "lady" that her great-granddaughter has become, but she would probably be able to pick her out in a roomful of Yankee cousins without hearing so much as a "yes'm" from the girl's lips. The idealized belle and lady have finally merged into a single symbol but, at the same time, both images have faded in the popular mind. Southern women now have many more options than their mothers and grandmothers had. Intelligence and educational accomplishments are now a matter of pride for women. Although grace and refinement are still cherished qualities,

2. Robb Forman Dew, "The Power and the Glory," in *A World Unsuspected: Portraits of Southern Childhood*, edited by Alex Harris (Chapel Hill: University of North Carolina Press, 1987), 119.

femininity no longer has to be maintained at the expense of direct competition between men and women. The ideal woman today is soft-spoken but assertive. She strives to achieve individual goals rather than to enhance the stature of her father, husband, or boss. The broader options that women now enjoy have put them in touch with the real rather than the mythical past of Southern women.

CHAPTER SIX

Southern Politics
Showtime to Bigtime

DAVID R. GOLDFIELD

Vice President George Bush worked the friendly crowd in Rocky Mount, North Carolina. Schoolchildren waved small American flags and cheered as he mounted the podium, flanked by the state's Republican U.S. senator, Jesse Helms, and Republican governor, Jim Martin. It was an uncompromisingly warm reception in a part of the state where registered Democrats outnumbered Republicans by nearly a two-to-one margin. Lee Atwater, the South Carolinian who ran the Bush presidential campaign, looked up nervously at the gray sky on that unseasonably cool, early September afternoon in 1988. The weather was Atwater's only concern that day. He was in friendly territory, registration figures or no. This would, in fact, be one of the vice president's few campaign visits to the South. After early October, he would not venture south again.

Why should he? By the 1980s, the South had become a Republican presidential preserve. Bush's energies were best spent in other, more hotly contested parts of the nation. In one sense, Bush was carrying on a lengthy Republican presidential tradition of campaigning lightly in the South. But whereas Republican presidential candidates before the 1950s had generally written off the South, George Bush was already counting the region in his win column. In less than a generation, the so-called Solid South had indeed become the Solid South; the only "detail" that had changed was party dominance. This change was part of a larger transformation of Southern politics since the 1950s, a shift that constitutes one of the most remarkable episodes in American political history.

Old South Roots

Charlotte journalist W. J. Cash wrote in his classic regional analysis, *The Mind of the South* (1941), that the twentieth-century South has "its tap root in the Old South." So it is with contemporary Southern politics. Seldom has a particular region blessed its nation with the quality of leadership offered by the South during the Republic's early years. The accomplishments of Washington, Jefferson, Madison, Marshall, and Monroe are well known, of course, but other luminaries such as South Carolina's Charles C. Pinckney and Virginia's George Mason commanded national respect and power as well.

But by the 1830s, the South had entered a period of decline in the national political arena. To be sure, it still boasted such major figures as South Carolina's John C. Calhoun and Henry Clay of Kentucky. But the quality and quantity of Southern leadership had begun to fade. Perhaps the hurly-burly of Jacksonian politics turned gentlemen-leaders away from politics; whereas formerly they had *stood* for office, now one had to *run* for office. Maybe the decline was merely following the law of averages, the region's incomparably good luck changing as leaders emerged from other parts of the country. But most of all it was due to slavery. The issue consumed the South and its leaders. Their energies became monopolized in a defense of the indefensible. Their voices became more shrill and less relevant with each passing year. As new free states entered the Union, Southern power declined in national councils. As early as 1831, Calhoun complained that the South was "a fixed and hopeless minority."

As slavery tore the nation apart, it also sundered the party system. By 1860 the Democratic party, the last of the major national parties, split into two parts. A new party, the Republican, had emerged in the preceding half-decade. But it was strictly a sectional party, almost all of whose adherents lived north of the Mason-Dixon Line. In addition it was a staunchly antislavery party. When the Republicans swept to victory in the 1860 election, the South could not abide the decision. Secession and civil war followed.

Reconstructing the Past: The Politics of Exclusion

During the war, Southern politicians followed a gentlemen's agreement to abandon party affiliation in the interests of unity. Parties disappeared in the South, but factionalism ran rampant, undermining the effectiveness of the Confederate central government. There were no strong leaders to transcend the incessant bickering that characterized Confederate administration. Able men sought glory on the battlefield, not in legislative halls.

The Reconstruction era witnessed the brief ascendancy of the Republican party in the South, a dominance built on the strength of federal arms, newly enfranchised freedmen, and Unionist whites. But Republican success was short-lived. Increasing dissatisfaction among the white population, confusion in Washington, and a growing lack of interest from other parts of the nation propelled the political opposition. Though the insurgents went by various names such as Conservatives or Redeemers, they were, by and large, Democrats. And it was to the Democrats that white Southerners looked as the party of redemption that would rescue their state and region from the party of General Sherman.

White Southerners were never a unified group, however. In the Old South, there had been sharp and occasionally bitter geographic divisions within states, as well as conflicts between slaveholders and nonslaveholders and between urban and rural interests. The war papered over some of these differences (though not all—the mountain areas remained loyal to the Union), but they resurfaced during the postwar decades. The strongest manifestation of white conflict was the Populist movement, which arose during the late 1880s and achieved some successes (occasionally by joining forces with the Republicans) in the early 1890s. Though the Populists attracted primarily tenants and sharecroppers, small landowners who felt squeezed by merchants, railroads, and the large plantation landlords also joined the movement. There were even scattered efforts to work with blacks. The Democratic party leadership successfully parried this deep thrust at their power base by adopting some of the milder programs of the Populists— or at least pretending to adopt them. The general prosperity of the South after 1896 also defused some of the more pressing economic issues. Finally, and most important, the Democrats took steps to eliminate blacks from the political process. Black disfranchisement accomplished several purposes. First, it eliminated a potential source of opposition against ruling Democrats. Second (though this idea was never stated publicly), the subtle methods employed to disfranchise blacks—a law stating explicitly that blacks could not vote would be unconstitutional—could also reduce the white electorate at the whim of the registrar. Between 1890 and 1907, Southern states revised their constitutions to include literacy tests, grandfather clauses (if your grandfather voted, you could too; because the grandfathers of most blacks had been slaves, the clause effectively eliminated the black vote), and understanding clauses (a prospective registrant was required to interpret a passage from the state or federal constitution). Though Democratic leaders assured their white constituents that these provisions would never be used against whites, dissenting or "troublemaking" whites sometimes found themselves without a ballot on election day.

As much as Southern whites abhorred black political power, it still may seem odd that they would support such schemes, which had the potential for considerable mischief. But Democratic leaders were successful in striking a bargain with their white constituents. In exchange for their support of black disfranchisement, whites would receive increased funding for public education and assurances that blacks would not become their economic competitors. The party also appealed to race pride, a time-honored political mechanism designed to bury dissent beneath the rhetoric of white supremacy. The plan worked, and it bound the South to a political system held together by racial inequalities.

A curious aspect of the Democrats' plan—at least to outsiders—was that it blended reaction (white supremacy) with progressivism (educational and electoral reform). The South participated in the national Progressive movement at the turn of the century, but strictly on its own terms. Southern local governments expanded services, but rarely to black districts. Such innovations in the political process as the commission form of government, wherein administrative responsibilities were divided among several elected commissioners, and the city-manager system, in which a nonpartisan, appointed manager administered a city's day-to-day operations, originated in the South. Some cities also introduced at-large elections to replace the ward or district system of representation. Not incidentally, these innovations also reduced the impact of the electorate on urban policy, either as voters or as members of interest groups.

The South's urban progressives also embraced city planning. As elsewhere, local governments used city planning to order the urban environment and, especially in the urban South, to ensure racial residential segregation (even though the U.S. Supreme Court struck down racial zoning in 1917). Southern city governments used their zoning power over the next half-century to protect white neighborhoods while allowing discordant land uses to invade and eviscerate black districts.

The Progressive movement in the urban South also reflected a combination traditional in Southern life: religion and politics. In the decades after the Civil War, it was sometimes difficult to separate church and state as public leaders actively sought religious endorsements and openly professed the theological tenets of evangelical Protestantism both on the stump and in office. This fervor was not surprising considering the overwhelming religious homogeneity of the region, in which over 90 percent of the population, black and white, adhered to one or another of the evangelical Protestant denominations. When religion merged with the Progressive desire to order the environment according to middle-class precepts, the results included a major campaign against alcohol and violations of the Sabbath. Prohibition and blue laws were the policy manifestations of this movement.

Eventually the merger of religion and politics carried over into a bitter battle fought during the 1920s over the teaching of evolution in public schools. Legislatures throughout the South vigorously debated whether or not to outlaw evolution in the classroom. Several states passed such statutes, including Tennessee, which became the site of the famous Scopes Monkey

Trial in Dayton in 1925. While the nation looked on in wonderment and derision, the citizens of eastern Tennessee acted out their morality play.

But the occasionally bizarre tendencies of Southern Progressivism should not obscure its positive accomplishments in educational reform, child-labor legislation, public health and sanitation measures, increased quality and level of urban services, and the creation of a social welfare bureaucracy. The leaders of these efforts frequently were not politicians but churchmen such as Episcopal minister Edgar Gardner Murphy and women such as Susan Pringle Frost.

Though conditions in the South during the first few decades of this century provided sufficient opportunities for a lifetime of dedicated reform, politicians rarely provided leadership in this area and only occasionally acceded to reform demands. The same paralysis that had gripped the antebellum Southern political system had overtaken its New South counterpart. The drive for white solidarity solidified race as *the* political issue. As political scientist V. O. Key, Jr., noted in his definitive study of Southern political culture, *Southern Politics in State and Nation* (1949), "In its grand outlines the politics of the South revolves around the position of the Negro." White supremacy was the glue that held the disparate white population together and, in turn, ensured the continued leadership of a relatively small coterie of politicians. The inclination in government was toward perpetuation, not innovation. Change was anathema to the political leadership. Not only was the electorate kept small, but state and local treasuries were as well. Low taxes and low service levels accompanied the opposition to change.

The one-party system reinforced the conservative nature of the Southern political process. Essentially, a relatively small group of Southern white males held political office for life, or until such time as they either tired of a particular political office or committed some great transgression that could not be ignored. Incumbents built up networks of friends, bureaucracies, and institutions that challengers found difficult to combat. For this reason, nearly one out of every three Democratic party primaries in the South during the first half of this century was uncontested. And, of course, the general election was almost always a one-person race. The Republican party receded toward oblivion, surfacing every four years to take advantage of federal patronage during a national Republican administration, but otherwise maintaining a very low local profile except in a few scattered mountain districts of North Carolina, Tennessee, and eastern Kentucky.

It is not surprising, given these conditions, that statewide political machines developed. Though we usually associate political machines with large cities, one-party politics generated bossism in rural areas as well. The most famous was the Byrd machine in Virginia, an organization that ruled the state for more than four decades after 1920. Though Harry Flood Byrd and his cohorts generally avoided the raucous racism of their political colleagues elsewhere, they followed a tight-fisted, low-service agenda. Similarly, the Barnwell Ring, composed of politicians from a twelve-county area in the South Carolina Low Country and led by Solomon Blatt, the son of Russian Jewish immigrants, dominated the Palmetto State's politics for more than a generation.

Showtime

The continued dominance of one party should not suggest that Southern politics during the first third of this century was mundane and boring. Though the faces rarely changed, the rhetoric was often entertaining, if not enlightening. Most Democratic primaries were contested. Because the primary was tantamount to a general election, it frequently drew a crowded field. As in the Old South, defense of race and region controlled and limited political discourse in the New South. Criticism implied disloyalty. Northerners had long been especially adept at South-bashing, and in the 1920s such criticism achieved the status of a low-art form in the person of Baltimore journalist H. L. Mencken.[1] Consequently, it was impolitic for a Southern politician to point toward illiteracy or poverty or infant mortality. And it was

---

1. A typical Mencken broadside: "for all its [the South's] size and all its wealth and all the 'progress' it babbles of, it is almost as sterile, artistically, intellectually, culturally, as the Sahara Desert."

not only impolitic but downright dangerous to discuss race relations in any except the crudest terms.

Accordingly, aspiring politicians became entertainers, traveling throughout the state or district, frequently with a band, often combining a political rally with a barbecue, and always engaging in rhetorical flourishes that dazzled more than they informed. Southern politicians historically were very good at oratory; it was part of their formal and informal education. The South was an oral, not a literary, culture. Traditions were passed down by word of mouth instead of through books, and the hot summer nights were more conducive to conversation than to reading. The advice that Jack Burden offered to Louisiana's novice gubernatorial candidate, Willie Stark, in Robert Penn Warren's novel *All the King's Men* (1946) was well taken:

Hell, make 'em cry, or make 'em laugh, make 'em think you're their weak and erring pal, or make 'em think you're God Almighty. Or make 'em mad. Even mad at you. Just stir 'em up, it doesn't matter how or why, and they'll love you and come back for more. Pinch 'em in the soft place. . . . Hell, their wives have lost their teeth and their shape, and likker won't set on their stomachs, and they don't believe in God, so it's up to you to give 'em something to stir 'em up and make 'em feel alive again. Just for half an hour. That's what they come for. Tell 'em anything. But for Sweet Jesus' sake don't try to improve their minds.

Followers of such advice made good stump speakers but lousy leaders. The highly factionalized, personalized political process characteristic of a one-party system produced an array of colorful characters, to be sure: South Carolina's one-eyed senator, "Pitchfork" Ben Tillman; the "Wild Ass of the Ozarks," Arkansas senator Jeff Davis; the Texas gubernatorial duo of "Ma" and "Pa" Ferguson, the former serving in the state house while the latter served in the state penitentiary; Mississippi's James K. Vardaman, the "White Chief" who campaigned in a white linen suit to match his shoulder-length white hair; his successor in Mississippi, Theodore "the Man" Bilbo, whose plan for black disfranchisement was to "visit" potential black voters on the night before the election; Alabama's "Kissin' Jim" Folsom, who toured the state with his "Strawberry Pickers" band and a big mop and wash bucket, vowing to sweep the "varmints" out of Montgomery; and the irrepressible Long family of Louisiana, with Huey crying "Every Man a King" and brother Earl escaping in his pajamas from a mental institution in Houston to resume duties as governor.

The rollicking nature of Southern politics, which straddled an uneasy line between good humor and buffoonery, also had a more serious side. When the entertainers entered office and their audiences disappeared, they were often unable or unwilling to cope with the numerous problems confronting their districts or states. Governors frequently were weaker than their legislatures, and the legislatures were comprised of part-time politicians and full-time lobbyists for the banking industry, public utilities, legal profession, insurance companies, soybean growers, tobacco manufacturers, and the like. Given the one-party system and the power of incumbency, there was little incentive for lawmakers to pay attention to individual citizens in distress, many of whom were black and could not vote in any case. As V. O. Key, Jr., summarized the situation, "The cold hard fact is that the South as a whole has developed no system or practice of political organization and leadership adequate to cope with its problems."

In Washington, Southern lawmakers functioned as the gatekeepers of tradition. Longevity brought key committee chairmanships. As late as 1964, Southern Democrats occupied 62.5 percent of Senate committee chairs, though they totaled only 31 percent of all Senate Democrats. These Southern committee chairmen scuttled or emasculated any legislation that might conceivably reduce their influence or threaten Southern customs. Presidents found their support necessary for the success of any legislative package. This was especially true of Democratic presidents who owed their election in great part to the Solid South. Simply put, the Democratic party needed the South. Prior to Franklin D. Roosevelt's election in 1932, Woodrow Wilson had been the only Democratic president in the twentieth century.

This lock on key positions does not mean that Southern congressmen wielded their power irresponsibly. During the New Deal era, they were among the staunchest supporters of Roosevelt's policies. Few Democrats, for example, matched Theodore Bilbo's loyalty to New Deal measures. Such loyalty was not surprising. The president (and his legislation) did not intend to upset Southern traditions. The twin objectives were to get business back on its feet and people back to work. In a federal system, the operation of many of the New Deal alphabet agencies depended on local bureaucrats who were part of the local Democratic party structure.

Cracks in the Solid South

If local Democratic organizations remained true to Southern customs, the national Democratic party was changing by the 1930s. Between 1900 and 1930, more than four million blacks had migrated from the South to the North. Though roughly 60 percent of the nation's blacks still resided in the South by 1930, this was down considerably from the 90 percent figure at the end of the nineteenth century. Many of the black migrants had settled in the larger cities of the North, where Democratic party machines welcomed their participation in the political process. Most blacks, of course, were nominally Republicans. But Democratic efforts in the urban North, combined with the popularity of New Deal programs, resulted in a major shift in black political support. In the 1936 election, for the first time ever, a majority of blacks voted for the Democratic presidential candidate. In addition, during the 1920s and 1930s the millions of immigrants who had entered the nation during the first two decades of the century were becoming naturalized citizens and were therefore eligible to vote. They were also concentrated in the larger cities of the North, and, like blacks, they were courted by the mostly Democratic political machines. Blacks and white ethnics were not only becoming important parts of the Democratic party but, because of their residence in states with large blocs of electoral votes, they were key figures in presidential politics. And as the influence of minority groups increased, the proportional influence of Southern Democrats declined.

Though racial discrimination in New Deal programs was widespread in the South, blacks throughout the region, especially in the cities, took heart at the federal presence. They recognized the power of their race in the North; they appreciated the attention of First Lady Eleanor Roosevelt; they noticed black appointments to federal positions; and they organized. Chapters of the

National Association for the Advancement of Colored People appeared all over the South, especially in the cities. The NAACP encouraged voter registration and filed suits protesting discriminatory practices. One such suit involved the petition of black Houston dentist Lonnie Smith, who challenged Texas's white primary law. Though Southern state constitutions could not explicitly discriminate against blacks, political parties could. The theory was that political parties were private clubs and thus had the right to admit only those of their choosing to membership and to participation in club activities. One of the activities of the Democratic party was the primary, and participation was limited to whites. Smith challenged this interpretation, claiming that the primary was a public election, not a private activity. In 1944 the U.S. Supreme Court upheld Smith's challenge in *Smith* v. *Allwright*, thus toppling one of the major political bastions of white supremacy in the South.

By 1944 many Southern Democratic politicians were alarmed at the liberal drift of the national Democratic party. Their concern was evident as far back as 1936, when South Carolina senator Ellison D. "Cotton Ed" Smith walked into the national Democratic party convention, saw a black minister offering the invocation, and exclaimed, "My God, he's black as melted midnight!" When a black congressman mounted the podium some time later, it was too much for "Cotton Ed," and he departed for South Carolina. For Smith and his colleagues, it was a startling revelation of the changing nature of the national Democratic party. Then came America's entrance into World War II, followed by the president's support for the Fair Employment Practices Committee and for black absentee voting in the armed forces. A disgruntled Democratic leader informed a *Fortune* magazine reporter touring the South in 1943, "If the Republican party would come out on the issue of white supremacy, it would sweep the South." These were strong words in a region where adherence to the Democratic party was taken as seriously as allegiance to God.

The 1944 presidential election marked the last time in the twentieth century that the South would go solidly Democratic. As the national Democratic party began to take on the policies and character of its now-dominant Northern wing, a split became inevitable. In response to the party's refusal to disavow President Truman's civil rights plank at the 1948 convention, most of the Southern delegates walked out and formed the States' Rights party (or "Dixiecrats," as they were more popularly known), which nominated South Carolina governor Strom Thurmond for president and Mississippi's Fielding Wright for vice president. The ticket fared poorly in the national election, failing to derail Truman's reelection bid and carrying only four Southern states: South Carolina, Mississippi, Alabama, and Louisiana. Not coincidentally, these were the only states that listed the Dixiecrat team under the Democratic party emblem. But the episode reflected the lengths to which Southern Democrats would go when challenged on white supremacy.

The Dixiecrat movement was a response not merely to national Democratic party policy but also to political events within the South. The Second World War triggered vast dislocations and migrations into and out of the South. Most movement occurred from farm to city, where the defense industries and training bases were usually located. Tens of thousands of Southerners, black and white, broke through the provincial veil and saw not only other parts of the country but other parts of the world. When they returned to their homes, they were no longer content with things as they were; they were open to new ideas and to new political attitudes. What could be described as a Southern political spring swept over the region in the years immediately following the war. New state political leaders emerged, including Georgia governor Ellis Arnall and Arkansas's Sid McMath, who were troubled both by the South's benighted image and by its reality. These political leaders represented even more serious challenges to the supremacy of the county courthouse cliques than did the Truman administration. Included in the new group were younger urban leaders who cared little about white supremacy but a great deal about industrial recruitment and economic development.

Even more ominous was the stirring of black political protest and power. By the mid-1950s, Southern blacks were primarily urban dwellers. Freed from the domination of rural white employers and political leaders, they joined Negro Voters' Leagues and began to register to vote despite the numerous obstacles. By the late 1940s, black voters were influential in many cities of the South, including Atlanta, Richmond, and Montgomery.

The South's traditional political leaders fought back by playing on the fear of black political power. Conjuring up a new Reconstruction era of black domination, they used the Truman administration's quest for civil rights legislation, the various court decisions that whittled away at white supremacy, culminating in the 1954 *Brown* ruling, and concern about Communist influences in the nation to restore their power by 1954. In the process, they routed the springtime politicians, reunited white voters, and moved once again to exclude blacks from the electoral process, with force if necessary. These politicians' disaffection with the national Democratic party was matched by their animosity toward the Republicans. After all, despite President Eisenhower's lukewarm endorsement of the *Brown* decision, he had sent the first federal troops since the Civil War into the South (to Little Rock in 1957), and he had supported the passage of the first two civil rights measures since Reconstruction. Southern politicians adopted the tactics of massive resistance at home and obstruction in Washington, stances that harked back to the years just before the Civil War.

The Republican Emergence

In the early 1960s Arizona's Republican senator, Barry Goldwater, saw an opening in the fortress of Southern politics for his party. The Republicans had narrowly lost the 1960 presidential election, thanks to a heavy black and ethnic turnout in the urban North that benefited John F. Kennedy and the Democrats. Though Kennedy also carried the South, it was not a solid victory. But his opponent, Vice President Richard M. Nixon, a card-carrying member of the NAACP, was not an appetizing political alternative. Indeed, the Democratic and Republican party platforms on civil rights differed little that year. Senator Goldwater felt that there was no point in the Republicans' competing for the black and ethnic vote in the North. During a press conference in Atlanta early in 1961, he advised his party to "go hunting where the ducks are," meaning among disaffected Southern whites. Goldwater was not necessarily suggesting that Republicans adopt racial demagoguery, but rather that, philosophically, the Republicans' tradition of limited government meshed well with Southern concerns about states' rights. Here was a common ground.

Armed with this so-called "Southern strategy," Goldwater carried five Southern states as the Republican presidential candidate in 1964—South Carolina, Georgia, Alabama, Mississippi, and Louisiana. Although he managed to win just one other state in the nation (Arizona), Goldwater accomplished what many political pundits had thought impossible a few short years earlier: conservative white Southerners in the most conservative part of the South walked into a voting booth and voted for the party of Lincoln, Grant, and Sherman. And when these Southerners walked out of the voting booth and did not hear the reproachful sound of J. E. B. Stuart's cavalrymen or the wails of their ancestors, the modern Southern Republican party was born.

Ironically, just as the Republican party of the 1850s was known as the white man's party in the North, so it came to be known as the white man's party in the South a century later. To Senator Goldwater, states' rights meant limits on federal power; to many of his new constituents, states' rights also meant white supremacy. The small Republican parties of the South, which had been relatively moderate on racial issues, were now inundated by new converts as a result of the national party's calculated strategy. In addition to changing and expanding the local Republican parties, the Southern strategy propelled black voters in the South (the majority of whom had voted for Eisenhower in 1956) into the Democratic party—the traditional party of white supremacy, the party of Bilbo, Vardaman, and, more recently, George Wallace.

In 1964 blacks were not yet a major force in Southern politics. With the passage of the Voting Rights Act in 1965, however, Southern blacks began to enter the political process in unprecedented numbers. Under the terms of the act, the federal government would ensure that no eligible black would be turned away from the registrar's table and that the Justice Department would keep a careful eye on electoral practices designed to eliminate or dilute the black vote, from at-large elections to changes in the location of polling places. Senator Goldwater's strategy appeared to be ill timed.

It soon became clear, however, that Southern black political power was more fanfare than fact. To be sure, the black electorate expanded dramatically, as did the number of black officeholders. But by the mid-1970s, the Southern electorate was still more than 80 percent white. Migration northward had mushroomed in the two decades following World War II, and the

South now contained only 50 percent of the nation's black population. More-over, this population was concentrated either in the larger cities or in rural areas of the Deep South. Many blacks were poor, and poor people generally tend to vote in lower numbers than more affluent citizens. While blacks flocked to the Democratic party, an even greater number of whites left, but they did not necessarily join the Republican party. In fact many, like the crowd greeting Vice President Bush in Rocky Mount, retained their Democratic registration. They did so from tradition or due to the simple fact that local Democratic candidates were sufficiently conservative for their tastes. South-ern white voters are intensely loyal, especially to their localities. Loyalty and localism will usually transcend party labels, particularly with respect to an incumbent. Between 1965 and 1985, for example, Republicans upset only one sitting Democratic governor in the South.

Though the Republicans continued to score successes among Southern whites at the presidential level—Gerald Ford managed to win a majority of the white vote against native son Jimmy Carter—their victories below that level remained unimpressive. Two-thirds of all state legislators in the South in 1980 were Democrats, for example. In four states—Alabama, Arkansas, Louisiana, and Mississippi—Democratic representation in state lawmaking bodies has not dipped below 90 percent in the twentieth century. The South-ern voter is not inherently schizophrenic. He or she is typically responding to Southern traditions of loyalty and conservatism, which favor neither the national Democratic party nor the local upstart Republican organization. The result is what political scientists John Van Wingen and David Valentine have called a "one-and-a-half, no-party system." The local dominance of the Democrats makes Southern politics a one-and-a-half-party system; the ab-sence of cohesive party structures due to the highly factionalized Democrats and the top-heavy Republicans makes it a no-party system as well. To put it more succinctly, the system reflects what political analyst Kevin Phillips terms "split-level realignment," though "dealignment" may be a better term, because Southerners are not necessarily shifting from the Democrats to the Republicans. In 1952 more than 75 percent of Southern voters claimed to be Democrats. By 1984 that identification had dropped dramatically to 40 percent. But the Republican party picked up only a small portion of the disaffected Democrats; only 19 percent of Southern voters in 1984 identified themselves as Republicans. The major increase occurred among Independents, who now account for one out of every three Southern voters.

Republicans obviously have been successful in courting these nonaligned voters as well as some Democrats, and not only in presidential races. Republicans point to numerous successes in U.S. Senate and House races, for example. One out of every three congressional representatives from the South is a Republican (including a majority of the Virginia delegation), and Republicans hold six out of twenty-two Senate seats. Another positive trend is in Southern state houses, where from 1930 to 1965 there was not one Republican governor. Between 1965 and 1986, Republicans won more than one out of every four gubernatorial races.

GOP leaders believe that both time and demography will extend these gains down to the local level. In just one short generation, the Southern electorate has changed markedly. In 1952 native whites comprised 83 percent of the Southern electorate, and the vast majority of blacks could not vote. By 1980 native whites accounted for only 57 percent of Southern voters, while those voters born outside the region comprised 26 percent of the electorate and blacks 17 percent. Migration from the North will continue, if not increase, and these newcomers tend to vote Republican by larger than a four to three margin.

But the Republicans do not necessarily have to count on a Yankee invasion to boost their prospects. Native Southern whites have changed since 1952 in much more than numbers. They are younger, with only dim memories, if any, of the Solid South generation and the cultural baggage that accompanied it. Although family traditions remain important in the South, it has become easier for sons and daughters to persuade their elders that a Republican vote more nearly honors those traditions than a Democratic one. Finally, today's Southerners are less likely to reside in rural areas and small towns, with the intense local loyalties they imply. These younger white voters are more footloose and much more likely to be living in metropolitan areas or in smaller communities along the ribbons of interstate highways. They are apt to be more middle class and less blue collar. The appeal of Republicans to these voters is due much less to race than to the free-enterprise, low-tax, low-social-service programs that Republicans historically have promoted nationwide. This profile adds up to a Republican gain, because the Democrats' major strength among Southern whites remains with those who are over fifty-five years of age, live in small towns, and work at blue-collar occupations—a diminishing proportion of the white electorate.

Black Ballots, White Power

What effect has the black vote had in this situation? Ninety-seven percent of black voters identify with the Democratic party—hardly a Republican advantage. Nonetheless, the strong identification of black voters with the Democrats has not been especially harmful to the GOP. For one thing, blacks comprise only 17 percent of the Southern electorate. For another, even though race is no longer the primary engine of Southern politics, the issue still motivates an undetermined number of white voters. The perception of the Democratic party as the party of blacks is not a positive one for some whites. The much-vaunted black voter registration gains in the 1970s and 1980s also spurred white registration. In fact, 90 percent of newly registered voters in the South during the 1970s were white.

This is not to deny the significance of the Voting Rights Act in mobilizing the Southern black electorate. The South leads the nation today in its number of black elected officials. Black mayors head such major cities as Atlanta and Richmond, as well as the bitter racial battleground of Birmingham (though white support for black candidates is typically less than 20 percent). More blacks in politics has meant better black services, more black construction contracts, and higher black employment in public sector jobs. The presence of the black vote has had a moderating, if not liberalizing, influence on Southern white politicians, the vast majority of whom supported the extension of the Voting Rights Act for another twenty-five years in 1982. Southern Democratic senators were prominent in the 1986 rejection of

Supreme Court nominee Justice Robert Bork: Alabama senator Howell Heflin, the chair of the Senate Judiciary Committee who owed his reelection to black votes (he received 44 percent of the white vote), was a key figure in scuttling the Bork nomination. As early as 1970, the black electorate helped to raise a new generation of Southern politicians to leadership as Reubin Askew of Florida, Dale Bumpers of Arkansas, and Jimmy Carter of Georgia all won their gubernatorial races.

Carter's election, in particular, typified the new era in Southern politics. He succeeded Lester Maddox, a die-hard segregationist. Even before his inauguration, Carter appointed the first black to the three-member Board of Pardons and Paroles. At his inauguration, the new governor announced that "the time for racial discrimination is over." And, as if to put history behind him and his state, the all-black Morris Brown College choir sang out with "The Battle Hymn of the Republic."

As important as these symbolic and rhetorical gestures were, they fell short of the promised transformation of black fortunes in the South. To be sure, the new leaders were instrumental in excising race-baiting from the Southern political process. But their main strengths were in promoting economic development and in administrative reform. As New York Times reporter Roy Reed summarized their accomplishments in 1974: "None of the new leaders has made real headway in providing industrial jobs for the multitudes of poor people who still live in the black belts. None has found the answers to newer problems such as urban blight and the growing concentration of economic power in fewer hands." Perhaps these issues were beyond the capabilities and resources of individual states. But there appeared to be a selective amnesia among the new breed of Southern governors, who said the right things but did much less.

Blacks also discovered that electing black officials did not necessarily ensure a new policy agenda, either. Most black officials presided over poor jurisdictions in the poorest regions of the South. Those in the larger cities, such as Atlanta mayor Andrew Young, often stressed economic development objectives and partnerships with the banking and mercantile communities. Young and others argued that such policies were necessary to foster competition with other cities and that prosperity benefited all, but the trickle-down theory still awaits a proof.

Finally, despite strong black adherence to the Democratic party, the black electorate is far from monolithic. There are growing policy differences between the expanding black middle class and the black underclass. One result of this estrangement has been a falling off in black voter participation—another setback for the Democratic party in the South.

New Voters, New Methods: Into the Bigtime

In recent years, new minorities have appeared in the Southern electorate, adding a new dimension to the political process. Hispanics had been prominent in urban Texas for decades, but only with the Voting Rights Act and the rise of neighborhood action groups did numbers translate into political power. The election of Henry Cisneros as mayor of San Antonio is merely one example of growing Hispanic visibility in the South. Even in Atlanta, there are 50,000 Hispanics and a like number of Koreans, Chinese, Indians, and Vietnamese. These new immigrants are adding a diversity to urban political life reminiscent of the political pluralism of Northern cities. In Miami, America's most Latin city, Hispanics comprise better than 54 percent of the population, and a Cuban, Xavier Suarez, is mayor. Though earlier immigrant groups in the urban North were overwhelmingly Democratic, the party affiliation of the new immigrants is not so easily discernible; in fact the Cubans are mostly Republicans.

The changing nature of political campaigns has also aided Republican ascendancy in the South. Gone are the days when candidates had to go to voters at "the forks of the creek," as V. O. Key, Jr., put it. There are fewer people at those forks now, and the ones that remain invariably have televisions. Few candidates running for statewide office can do without media consultants. The thirty- or sixty-second advertisement has become the major conduit to the electorate, and, ironically, campaigns often revolve around personality as much as they did in the showtime days of Southern politics.

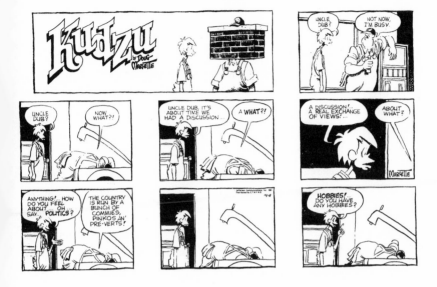

Republican candidates who lack extensive local networks can reach their constituents through television. In addition, the cost of media campaigns has meant that politics in the South (and elsewhere, of course) has become primarily a pastime of the wealthy and their friends. Generally, Republicans have had better access to wealthy circles than have Democratic candidates. Black candidates are at a further disadvantage.

With all of these positive attributes—demography, economics, process, and ideology—it is surprising that the Republicans remain the minority party in the region. While a new Solid South may be forming in terms of Republican dominance in presidential politics, Democrats reign supreme at the local and state levels (especially in the Deep South states of Georgia, Alabama, Mississippi, and Louisiana, where the black population is larger than in other parts of the South). Traditions still count in the South, and the sense of loyalty to place and past continue to favor the Democrats. The challenge will be for the Democrats to find a way to translate these traditions into an agenda that suits the changing electorate in the South. Black and white Southerners are so divergent in terms of their political views—their perceptions of the government's responsibility to provide jobs and social services, to take one major example—that statewide Democratic candidates must engage in a "tight-rope act," as political scientist Alexander P. Lamis puts it, convincing whites of their fiscal conservatism and blacks of their social conscience. By and large, they have performed successfully. The difficulty with Democratic presidential candidates is that they rarely appreciate this balance, and hence Democrats have failed to carry the South in five out of the last six presidential elections.

Southern politics reflects the vast changes that have occurred in the South over the past generation. The participation of blacks, the in-migration of Northerners, and the increasing urbanization of the electorate indicate the social and economic transformation of the region. White supremacy is no longer the glue of the political process, and, though political analysts continue to debate what has replaced it, the one-party system has likewise disappeared. Leaders from both parties plot their Southern strategies, testifying to the increasing importance of the South on the national scene. With one-third of the nation's electoral vote, Southern politics has gone bigtime. Yet in politics, as with most other changes in the region, the South still remains. Religion intrudes (sometimes uncomfortably) into politics; "friends-and-neighbors" politics still counts for more than party affiliation; a strong streak of individualism and distrust of government prevails; and race continues to play a role in the system, albeit at a lower profile. So it remains that the best way to understand Southern politics is by understanding Southern history.

Uncle Sam's Other Province
The Transformation of the Southern Economy

D A V I D R. G O L D F I E L D &

T H O M A S E. T E R R I L L

It's a good life here in the South. Salaries may be a bit lower than in other parts of the country, but the trade-off is worth it. That trade-off is the lifestyle: the generously landscaped suburban subdivisions, the proximity to mountains and beaches, the climate-controlled comfort of new buildings, new homes, and new shopping malls. The pace is slower; the clerks at the mall take a little more time with each customer; the bank teller knows you by your first name; and the mechanic at the neighborhood filling station will fix your car and you will still have enough money left over to eat for the rest of the week. This is the Sunbelt, y'all—a land where prosperity has not yet driven out civility. True, traffic jams are prodigious, pollution is getting worse, and occasionally a note of irritability creeps into the otherwise sweet music of Southern conversation. But, as one Floridian noted, "It beats the hell out of pellagra."

For those of us who have come here since 1960 or were born here since then (and, according to statistics, that is most of us), it seems difficult to understand how, just a half-century ago, the federal government anointed the South as the nation's "Number One economic problem." How and why did this transformation take place? How did the nation's perennial ugly duckling become the sleek, contented swan?

Agriculture's Legacy

As with most questions about the South, the answers lie in the region's history. In the decades before the Civil War, the South was an exceedingly prosperous place. Cotton was king, and it was a benevolent monarch to the white Southerners who planted it. Only the millionaire merchant-princes of New York could match the homes, the furnishings, the travel, and the lavish entertainment undertaken by King Cotton's retainers in such areas as the Mississippi Delta. Those who made their living from other staples such as rice, tobacco, or sugar also found that the climate and soil favored their enterprises. The wealthiest rice grandee was Nathaniel Heyward, owner of over 1,600 slaves in the Combahee River region of South Carolina. At his death in 1851, his property was worth approximately $2.5 million.

To be sure, agriculture was not the only lucrative enterprise in the Old South. William Gregg's Graniteville, South Carolina, cotton mill and Joseph R. Anderson's Tredegar Iron Works in Richmond would have been prominent businesses in any region. And not everyone in agriculture fell into the categories of planter or slave. A majority of the South's farmers, in fact, owned no slaves at all. They cultivated a little cotton or tobacco or some surplus corn and tended livestock. But it was the plantation, above all else, that made the Old South wealthy.

There were a few economic problems that concerned Southerners, especially as sectional controversy heated up after 1850. Despite their wealth, Southerners were dependent on Northern credit, shipping, and distribution. A related concern was that the South seemed little inclined to remedy this dependence. Investments continued to pour into land and slaves as opposed to shipbuilding, railroad construction, and industry. Though the South began to diversify its investments in the 1850s, the Civil War underscored the thin base of the region's economy. The North controlled 90 percent of the country's industry and had twice as many miles of railroad track as the South. By late 1863, the economic situation in the Confederacy was desperate. One North Carolinian advised his soldier brother to desert "to the other side where you can get plenty and not stay in this one horse, barefooted, naked, and famine stricken Southern Confederacy." It is amazing that the South mobilized as well as it did and kept up the fight for four long years when, on paper at least, the war was no contest.

But the Civil War was just a prelude to the decades of poverty that lay ahead for the South. The Southern land was devastated, a worthless currency thrust the region into financial chaos, railroads were vandalized, slaves were freed and left the plantations, and Union officials had seized thousands of cotton bales. Desperate for cash, Southerners turned to their old staple, cotton, with a vengeance. In 1860 the South produced 3.8 million bales of cotton; by 1900 production had reached almost 8.5 million bales. Tobacco cultivation also increased, doubling by 1900 and expanding into new areas.

In order to maintain that prodigious cotton production, new labor arrangements emerged. Most freedpeople became sharecroppers, working out yearly contracts under which landowners customarily furnished housing and fuel in exchange for a share (usually one-half) of the crop cultivated by the tenants. But sharecroppers received their payments only once a year when they sold their shares of the crop. How were they to survive in the meantime? The answer was credit. Local merchants set up shop (often they were themselves large landowners) to supply sharecroppers with food, seed, and other necessities in exchange for a promise of payment once the tenants sold their crops. Accounts were settled at harvest time. The law of supply and demand, however, worked against the sharecropper.

Cotton was the only sure-fire cash crop in many parts of the South, and so sharecroppers devoted most of their land to its cultivation. Soon supply outstripped demand and the farmers had to grow still more cotton to cover falling prices that, in turn, sent prices down further, and this, in turn, necessitated increased cotton production, and so on. By 1890 sharecroppers were singing a sad refrain: "Five-cent cotton / Forty-cent meat / How in the heck can a poor man eat?" The result was that sharecroppers found it difficult to get out of debt. Unable to obtain credit elsewhere, they found themselves in a state of peonage or debt servitude. Slavery, in effect, had returned in another guise. Some merchants helped the process along by cooking the books—many of their debtors were illiterate. Blacks were not alone in this state of poverty. Many white farmers also became indebted to merchants, lost their land, and became tenants or sharecroppers. King Cotton had become a despot.

King Cotton's subjects settled into a difficult life: rural isolation, few social services, hardly any labor-saving machinery, dreadful heat in the summer, and inadequate diets. John Andrew Rice, a South Carolina writer, remembered the ordeal of picking cotton as a fourteen-year-old around 1900. He wrote that "besides backbreaking toil, September was presently around us, the worst time of the year. Food began to run low; pork by now was rancid, cabbage was burned by the heat of the sun and collards had not yet felt the sweetening touch of frost, turnips were tasteless and beans rattled in the pod. This was the time of dysentery; heat-weary bodies became so ill that they could barely drag themselves out of bed to do the necessary tasks for keeping alive, and still work had to be done."

Sharecroppers, white and black, subsisted on the 3-M diet—meat (fatback), meal (cornbread), and molasses (sorghum). They seldom saw a doctor and suffered from malaria, hookworm, and/or pellagra. Midwives delivered their children, and infant mortality was high. Mostly illiterate, they lived in cheap clapboard shacks that lacked plumbing and, often, glass windowpanes. Many of these homes even lacked outdoor privies.

The Industrial Alternative

Some Southern leaders were determined that if they had their way, there would be an alternative to the downward spiral of sharecropping—at least for the whites. Atlanta journalist Henry W. Grady was fond of regaling post–Civil War audiences, North and South, with a story about a North Georgia funeral he had attended. The coffin, the hearse and the mules drawing it, the shovel that dug the grave, the marble marker, the minister's Bible, the clothes for the deceased—all were produced outside the South. Only the corpse and the hole in the ground were local. Grady's point was, "We have got to go to manufacturing to save ourselves."

The cure, though, may have been worse than the disease. One of the first developments came in the lower South, where during the 1880s state governments, desperate for cash, offered huge tracts of timberland and mineral deposits to outside speculators for a song. Extensive land sales caused lumber production to boom along the Gulf Coast in what one government forestry expert called "probably the most rapid and reckless destruction of forests known to history."

In Birmingham, Henry De Bardeleben captured the city's steel-making enterprises during the 1880s, proclaiming, "I was the eagle and I wanted to eat up all the craw-fish I could—swallow up all the little fellows, and I did it." De Bardeleben was soon swallowed by John H. Inman, a railroad magnate who, in turn, was swallowed by J. P. Morgan in 1907. Another indigenous industry had gone north.

Another Southern entrepreneur, James B. Duke, mused to himself, "If John D. Rockefeller can do what he is doing for oil, why should I not do it in tobacco?" He crushed one competitor after another and in 1890 merged his holdings into the American Tobacco Company. He moved his headquarters to New York City and set out to capture a large share of the world's tobacco-manufacturing market.

Not all Southern enterprises eventually ended up in Northern hands or in Northern offices. By 1900 the Atlanta-based Coca-Cola Company was selling more than 370,000 gallons of its "refreshingly delicious" beverage and promoting its value as a "pick-me-up"—a valid claim since the drink allegedly contained a small amount of cocaine, hence its early twentieth-century nickname of "dope." Within a decade, Asa Candler's company had nearly six million gallons in sales annually, some to foreign countries. In Nashville at about the same time, the appropriately named Joel O. Cheek was experimenting with coffee beans. In those days, consumers were accustomed to purchasing one grade of bean and grinding it at home. Cheek's idea was to blend various grades and grind the beans. His ground blend was tasty but expensive, and so in order to market his new product, he asked Nashville's finest hotel, the Maxwell House, to serve his coffee. In exchange Cheek put the hotel's name on the label. In 1907 President Theodore Roosevelt visited the Maxwell House and dined with Cheek and a few other business leaders. As the president drained his coffee cup, he turned to his companions and remarked that the coffee was "good to the last drop." Thus a popular coffee and a memorable advertising slogan were born.

In its economic and social impact, the most important homegrown industry was textiles. With all the cotton being grown, all the cheap labor barely scraping by on the farm, and all the water power waiting to be harnessed, textile manufacturing was a natural enterprise for the South. The Piedmont, an area extending from Richmond through the Carolinas and north Georgia and ending just south of Birmingham, had the readiest access to cotton, labor, and power, and by the turn of the century the region was responsible for more than half of all the textile output in the United States.

Textile mill villages sprouted up and down the Piedmont, providing work for hard-pressed, often landless farm families. The growth of mill villages led to two new classes of Southerners, the mill hands and the mill owners. By 1900 these classes were established in self-contained communities, most located outside town limits to escape taxes, town control, and temptation for the workers. The workday was long, wages were low, and conditions in the mill—high heat and humidity in the summer and damp cold in the winter— were unhealthy. But the alternatives on the farm weren't much better. At the mill, there were paying jobs for entire families, including children as young as ten, and the workers often developed a feeling of community solidarity.

This does not mean that they endured cotton mill life without complaint. One of the great myths of the South is that its white work force was docile. On the contrary, there were a number of bloody strikes during the 1920s and 1930s, as well as occasional work stoppages or slowdowns. Nevertheless, unions made few inroads in the Southern textile mills. Owners were able to marshal community institutions against organized labor, and the workers themselves were well aware of the overabundance of labor and the alternative life on the farm should management retaliate. When the Congress of Industrial Organizations (CIO) launched "Operation Dixie" in 1946, one minister reminded his congregation that CIO stood for "Christ Is Out." Companies and local chambers of commerce circulated a cartoon of a union representative with Negroid features who carried a carpetbag labeled "CIO," saying, "I've come down here to organize you bastards." Opponents equated union organizers with communists, and their techniques were usually successful.

" REMEMBER WHEN THEY USED TO SEND US POVERTY PROGRAMS!..."

As late as 1960, when 81 percent of the South's rubber workers belonged to unions, only 14 percent of the region's textile workers were organized.

Climbing Out: Depression and War

When the Great Depression struck, many parts of the South scarcely knew it—they had been depressed for so long it seemed impossible to sink lower. Most Southerners had not shared in the prosperity of the 1920s. In fact, for only the second decade in the history of the South (the other was the 1860s), per-capita income went down. No other region in America has ever suffered a decade-long decline in income. So the depression had little impact on the standard of living of many Southerners. A tenant farmer in Mississippi remembered that he had heard about the economic crisis of 1929, but that the only real impact it had on his family was that it "increased the fear a little bit of maybe not being able to get any food at all."

The New Deal offered some help, but for thousands of small farmers, tenants, and sharecroppers, the government's Agricultural Adjustment Act (AAA) was disastrous. The basic idea behind the AAA was sound: take millions of acres out of cotton cultivation, raise cotton prices, and pay landowners for the acres they did not cultivate. Though the act stipulated that landowners should share these payments with sharecroppers and tenants, many owners summarily dismissed them. Assisted by cheap, government-subsidized loans and crop-reduction payments, large farm operators shifted to more mechanized, less labor-intensive agriculture. Small farmers who had somehow managed to hold on to their land through the prolonged agricultural depression now found that they could not compete with mechanized cultivation.

The Tennessee Valley Authority (TVA) and the Rural Electrification Administration (REA) were more helpful to rural Southerners. In the 1930s, less than 5 percent of the farms in the South had electricity. (The national average was 14 percent.) Russell Baker of the *New York Times* remembered that women in the rural area of northern Virginia where he was born kept house during the 1930s in much the same way as women had before the Civil War. Lacking electricity—and gas, telephones, automatic laundries, vacuum cleaners, refrigerators, radios, plumbing, and indoor toilets—they "toiled like a serf." For instance, washing and ironing clothes was an arduous weekly task that took the better part of two days. Doing the laundry involved chopping wood, toting water and boiling it, scrubbing the clothes by hand, rinsing and wringing them, emptying and refilling tubs, drying and starching clothes, then ironing them with flatirons heated on wood stoves in furnace-hot kitchens. Backed by the REA and the TVA, electricity came to the rural South during the decade or so after 1935. Its advent transformed domestic life, facilitated the mechanization of agriculture, and encouraged industrial expansion.

Despite these improvements, most Americans in 1940 viewed Jeeter Lester as the typical Southerner. A character in Erskine Caldwell's novel *Tobacco Road*, Lester lived in abject poverty and ignorance in a one-room shack near Augusta, Georgia. The Lesters had seventeen children, and all but two of the twelve surviving offspring lived somewhere else. Lester was not sure where they or any of his several grandchildren were. He was forever vowing to get started on something—a crop, selling firewood, an operation for his hare-lipped daughter. He finally did start a fire in a nearby field to clear it for cultivation, but the wind drove the fire into the Lester house, and the sleeping family was burned alive. The popularity of *Tobacco Road* underscored the widespread perception that the South was "Uncle Sam's Other Province."

But World War II began to change both the image and the reality of the South. If the Sunbelt had a particular origin, it was the war (in fact, in 1940 the Air Force referred to the area below the 37th parallel as the "sunshine belt"). The federal government invested $7 billion in the region in military bases and industrial plants; private investors added $1 billion to that. Income payments rose 250 percent during the war, and one-fourth of that money came from the federal government. A reporter for *Fortune* magazine interviewed an erstwhile sharecropper, now a defense worker in a Panama City, Florida, plant, whose newfound affluence had created an unanticipated dilemma: "Hit's got me right bothered," the worker allowed, "how I'm a-goin' to spend it all." The tidal wave of money lifted the South out of its long depression.

Employment opportunities in Southern cities also relieved the pressures on the farm. The South's farm population declined by 22 percent during the war, further stimulating mechanization and crop diversification, which, in turn, boosted farm income. Between 1940 and 1944, farm income in the South more than doubled. By the end of the war, progress and prosperity had created strange scenes in the rural South. Writer H. C. Nixon observed in 1945 that, in his native Calhoun County, Alabama, farmers were using "three kinds of power for plowing: tractor, mule, and ox," and they went to town "in wagons, buggies, and autos." In winter farmers heated their homes with "pine knots, oak wood, coal, oil, gas, and electricity."

Preparing for the Sunbelt

But would a peacetime economy sustain the wartime achievements? The answer was a resounding "Yes!" Military installations became larger and more permanent during the cold war, particularly the uranium processing facilities at Oak Ridge, Tennessee, and the expanded naval and ship-building facilities at Newport News, Norfolk, Charleston, Tampa, Mobile, Pascagoula, New Orleans, and Houston. An aircraft-manufacturing plant at Marietta, Georgia, later evolved into the giant Lockheed-Georgia operation.

Politics played a large role in the persistence of wartime prosperity. A half-century of one-party rule had left Southern Democrats dominant in Congress, especially in the Senate. The high-seniority delegations from the South occupied key positions on major committees. During the years immediately following World War II, Senator Richard B. Russell, chairman of the Senate Appropriations Committee, was probably the most powerful individual in that house. Russell's fellow Georgian Carl Vinson headed the Armed Services Committee in the House of Representatives. These two legislators were instrumental in securing for their state fifteen military installations that employed more than 40,000 people, as well as funneling lucrative defense contracts to Lockheed in Marietta, making that firm the largest nongovernmental employer in the state. By 1960 these facilities contributed $2 billion annually to Georgia. Charleston's congressman, L. Mendel Rivers, performed like services for his constituents, leaving one journalist to express wonder that the weight of all those military installations had not caused the genteel seaport to sink.

That ubiquitous Southern type, the booster, silenced momentarily by the depression, erupted with renewed vigor after World War II. While fending off unions with one hand, they extended the other to Northern investors. The difference between this and earlier eras is that postwar efforts were usually organized with strong state and local government assistance. The economic recruitment operation in Georgia was one example. During the early 1950s, the Georgia Power Company, the Georgia Municipal Association, and the Georgia Institute of Technology's Engineering Experiment Station combined to sponsor the Certified City Program. This program assisted local leaders with civic improvements ranging from landscaping to developing educational and recreational facilities in order to enhance the town or city's attractiveness to outside industries. The South's important selling point was that its environment and amenities could be enjoyed by those businesses for whom such advantages had long ago disappeared—if, in fact, they had ever existed. And, not incidentally, they could be enjoyed in the context of the low taxes and low wages for which the South had always been noted.

Southern governors went on the offensive to advertise their states as good places to do business. By 1960 North Carolina governor Luther Hodges had logged 67,000 miles seeking investors, including tenants for a new concept: the Research Triangle Park, to be located between Raleigh, Durham, and Chapel Hill. Hodges hoped that the concentration of highly trained individuals attracted to the area by the major universities and medical centers there would serve as a draw for research and development firms. His hunch proved correct, though not immediately. The park eventually sustained Hodges's faith and became a prototype for similar high-tech agglomerations across the country. By the 1970s, Southern governors were making forays to the capitals of Europe and the Far East as easily as they had traveled to Pittsburgh and Cleveland.

Other aspects of the South's postwar economic development required less lobbying and advertising. Florida had benefited from its balmy climate since early in the century, but as roads improved and as retirement there became economically more feasible for more people after the war, the Sunshine State enjoyed an unprecedented boom. Also, by the mid-1950s the Texas-Louisiana area was producing one-half of the nation's oil, with the richest deposits yet untapped. The abundance of oil and natural gas, sulfur, and fresh water was ideal for the development of petrochemicals.

By the 1960s, the South was poised to build on its postwar foundation of growth and development. Regional and national events coalesced during that turbulent decade to restore the South, at long last, to the head of the economic development class. The difference from the previous century's economic prosperity, however, was that, rather than being based on one or two agricultural staples, the new economy was diverse and located in the metropolitan South. King Cotton had abdicated, so to speak, and a more democratic economy stood in its place.

The Sunbelt

Although numerous white Southerners doubted it at the time, the 1964 Civil Rights Act and the Voting Rights Act of 1965 were the biggest boons to economic development in the region since the invention of the cotton gin. The nation's stormy love-hate relationship with the South had taken a turn for the worse in the early 1960s. Challenges to white supremacy such as the Freedom Rides of 1961 and the Birmingham desegregation demonstrations in 1963 provoked bloody responses that revulsed the nation. The days of dogs and hoses became etched deeply into the national collective consciousness. But the decisive federal legislation in mid-decade spread like a rainbow across the once-stormy region and considerably brightened the South's dark image in the minds of Americans. It didn't hurt that, within days of President Johnson's signing of the Voting Rights Act, a vicious race riot erupted in the Watts district of Los Angeles, touching off a four-year frenzy of racial strife that ultimately paled the South's dilemma by comparison. The adverse racial publicity now came not from Selma, but Detroit; not from Birmingham, but Newark.

Equally important in the South's rehabilitation was a change in lifestyles. The construction of a national interstate highway network, an increase in disposable income, a lengthening of vacation time, and a decrease in the average retirement age put people on the move. The sense of tradition and history offered by the South was a stark contrast to the uncertainty that existed elsewhere in the nation during the sixties.

It was not just old buildings that Americans sought in the South, but a lost lifestyle. The cities in this urban nation had become shabby and dangerous places, where tempers and budgets were chronically short. The traffic jammed, the pace grew ever more frantic and pointless, and the taxes were more onerous. In the South, however, even in the urban South, the pace was, as Rosemary Daniell noted, "somewhere between Guatemala and New York," and descriptions of Southern cities heavily emphasized the "shady live oaks and the prodigious banks of azaleas."

Even more subtle Southern elements operated on the American consciousness in the 1960s. When Americans read, for example, they often read

Southerners. Thomas Wolfe, William Faulkner, Robert Penn Warren, and Eudora Welty were on everyone's reading lists. These writers' themes varied, of course, but the intrusion of the modern world into insular societies and the moral dilemmas confronting individuals who were both victims and beneficiaries of this conflict were common threads. Most Americans outside the South had passed through the gates of whatever characterized late-twentieth-century life, and it was edifying to discover, even in fiction, a civilization where the choices were not inevitable and irrevocable, where it was still possible to place each foot in a different era without the straddle becoming painful.

The good stories told by Southern writers translated well into television and theatrical film adaptations. "Roots," of course, became one of the most-watched television series of all time. Movies with Southern themes were hardly new in the 1960s—*Gone with the Wind* and *Jezebel* had captured national audiences a generation earlier, and the former enjoyed a big come-back in later years. By the early 1970s, the "Southern" was as distinctive a film genre as the Western. *In the Heat of the Night* (1967), starring Sidney Poitier as a Philadelphia police detective and Rod Steiger as the prototypical Mississippi sheriff, initiated Hollywood's new version of the modern South, exemplified by Steiger's warming to his black colleague by the picture's end.

In fact, by the early seventies, the formerly dreaded, paunchy Southern sheriff had become almost an impish character in the media's portrayal. Chrysler Corporation employed a down-home sheriff type to sell Dodge automobiles: his closing words were, "Y'all be careful, now, heah!" Also in the early 1970s, *Spencer's Mountain* (1961), a novel by Earl Hamner, Jr., became the basis for CBS-TV's "The Waltons." Southern blacks evolved from victims or Sambos into heroes (which threatened to become another stereotype) in *Sounder* (1972) and in the television adaptation of "The Autobiography of Miss Jane Pittman" (1974). Finally, the South became the repository of the macho, law-and-order, good-guy type in a nation anxiously seeking straightforward heroes. *Walking Tall* (1972), the biographical portrayal of Tennessee sheriff Buford Pusser, and the Burt Reynolds vehicle *White Lightning* (1973) provided action and happy endings for all.

If the South emerged in American literary and film preferences as the region closest to the heart, Southern music generated a loyal following for many of the same reasons. Country music was the people's music, and its lyrics reflected a deep attachment to place, especially for those transplanted Southerners working on railroads, on chain gangs, or "up North." Its themes were the wanderlust, yet rootedness, that permeated everyday Southern life; loves lost and won; and families held together by faith and fortitude or torn apart by infidelity, death, or leave-takings. The lyrics told stories because, in the oral tradition of the plain folk, storytelling was an important means of communication and entertainment. The national popularity of country music in the troubled sixties and seventies owed much to the passing of these oral traditions from an electronic America as well as to the simplicity and forthrightness of the lyrics and melodies in a time of ambiguity and uncertainty. In 1971 New York City surrendered to the national trend when radio station WHN shifted to a country format and the Lone Star Cafe became the habitat of the button-down crowd.

So the South was "in," as far as the national consciousness was concerned, long before Jimmy Carter's election sent Yankees running to their dictionaries or to the foreign food sections of their supermarkets to locate grits. The South was taken to the nation's heart again, not only for its music and literature, but also for its lifestyle and its economic promise. The relaxed pace had been there all along, of course, but always with the rough edge of frontier primitivism showing through—a gap-toothed poverty of mind and body, a kudzu-covered, rusty Chevrolet. But now the South was clean and shiny, with a new veneer of glass and steel, indoor plumbing, and air-conditioning. The South was now the repository of the "good life," having changed from the nation's "Number One economic problem" to the Promised Land in a generation. At a time when the American pursuit of happiness was coming a cropper in the ghettos of Northern cities, in the rice paddies of Vietnam, and on college campuses—a time when everyone, it seemed, was angry about something—the South appeared to be a happy place. As Walker Percy observed in his 1966 novel, *The Last Gentleman*:

> The happiness of the South was very formidable. It was an almost invincible happiness.... Everyone was in fact happy. The women

were beautiful and charming. The men were healthy and successful and funny. . . . They had everything the North had and more. They had a history, they had a place redolent with memories, they had good conversation, they believed in God and defended the Constitution, and they were getting rich in the bargain. They had the best of victory and defeat.

This doesn't mean that Northerners unequivocally opened their hearts and minds to the South. Some of the fascination for the region resulted from the traditional perception that the South's distinction was less admirable than exotic (and even grotesque). Numerous Northern transplants reported receiving the commiseration of friends and relatives when they broke the news of their transfer to the South. Food and reading material soon followed.

But whatever the perception, more Northerners than ever were choosing the South as a place to live, work, raise children, and retire. Much as the nation had trekked to the American West with high hopes and a glimmer in its eyes a century earlier, so now Americans finally heeded Henry Grady's call of a century earlier: "Southward this star of empire." The South's population increased by more than 7 million during the 1960s, the largest growth in the nation, and by the early 1970s the South had become the country's most populous region, holding more than one-third of America's people. During the 1960s, for the first time in a hundred years, more people moved into the South than out of it.

The newcomers fueled an unprecedented growth in employment. In the decade after 1965, the South's employment base grew by 22 percent, compared with a national average of 12 percent. The service sector and government employed nearly half of all Southern jobholders, with manufacturing a distant third at 16 percent. The South was moving rapidly into the postindustrial era with scarcely a backward glance at its brief industrial history. The South, in effect, bypassed the industrial age and leaped directly into a service economy—Birmingham and some sectors of the furniture and textile industries were exceptions—avoiding for the most part the burdens of a cumbersome and expensive industrial infrastructure. The "quality" of the in-migrants was high because such service activities as banking, insurance, and government and corporate administration required well-educated, skilled individuals. This influx, in turn, spurred consumer demand and generated new service-sector activities.

The media warmed to the southward trend. A series of articles in the *New York Times* during February 1976, followed in March by a *Time* magazine cover story entitled "Americans on the Move," embedded the Sunbelt in the national consciousness. These stories were often juxtaposed with photographs and articles depicting the blustery, decaying, crime-ridden cities of the North. The building crane was the most-photographed feature on the Southern landscape, and "help wanted" was heard as commonly as "sir" and "ma'am." Houston's mayor, Fred Hofheinz, summarized the feeling for the *Times* in 1976: "The South and Southwest are frontiers of the new industrial America, where people can still reach the American dream. This is the new Detroit, the new New York. This is where the action is."

Some Northerners, especially public officials, were more alarmed than impressed by the sudden burst of Sunbelt prosperity. They charged Southern business and political leaders with piracy and unfair competition. But the image of firms picking up lock, stock, and payroll and moving south was inaccurate. Most of the Sunbelt economic growth came from branching, from the emergence of home-grown enterprises, and from the businesses created or expanded to service these new firms.

The South's economic growth generated its own momentum. Skill levels rose, as did wages. Universities expanded and the quality of curricula and faculties increased. The cultural activities common in Northern cities, such as fine arts museums, symphony orchestras, and ballet and opera companies, appeared and expanded, and branches of major enterprises soon followed, from IBM to McDonald's hamburgers. These services and activities in turn attracted more retirees. Florida had perennially led the nation in the "mailbox economy"—characterized by tens of thousands of retirees who received their checks from Northern states and pension funds—but during the seventies other Southern states, including the Carolinas, Virginia, and areas along the Gulf Coast, became retirement havens as well.

The rate of growth slowed somewhat in the 1980s, but the South continued to move into the national economic mainstream. Incomes reached about 90 percent of the national average. The new middle class—people in administrative, managerial, clerical, technical, or professional positions—became a numerical majority in the South in 1980. Agricultural output more than doubled in the decade after 1975, but the ranks of farmers diminished to about 1 million, compared to the 13 million who had tilled the soil in 1940.

Remnants from the Legacy: Shadows over the Sunbelt

Amid the Sunbelt hoopla, there are troubling reminders that economic development has not necessarily transformed the South into a warmed-over North. Remnants of the old economic regime are not easily purged, even if they are obscured by the skyscrapers and megamalls. The Sunbelt is primarily a metropolitan phenomenon, an economy confined to the interstates and rarely penetrating the back roads. By the mid-1970s, although rural Southerners comprised just slightly more than one-third of the region's population, they accounted for 55 percent of its poor. Unemployment in the rural South is 37 percent higher than in the urban centers. As Representative Larry Walker of rural Perry, Georgia, put it, "I've heard that if you take Atlanta out of Georgia, we're not doing as well as Mississippi."

When one drives down those back roads, maybe not even paved and where the electricity pole has not yet come, the houses—or more properly shacks— are distinguished by sagging porches, broken windows covered over by cardboard, and rusted tin roofs. "And you think oh God," wrote journalist Joel Garreau, "please don't let there be anybody living in that; please let it be abandoned. But a line of laundry flutters out back." Blacks account for a large portion of the rural poor. Better than two out of three black children in the rural South in 1983 lived in poverty; for black rural children under age six, the figure was an incredible 80 percent. Black women in the rural South had a poverty rate of 58 percent—more than one-and-a-half times as high as the rate for white women.

In the bad old days, the rural or small-town resident could supplement an income scratched from the soil with so-called "public work" at the local mill or factory. But that type of public work is fast disappearing from the rural South, moving overseas in search of still cheaper labor or closing down altogether. Lacking the amenities of the fast-improving metropolitan areas, the rural South cannot compete in the changing economic climate. Its small towns often resemble the one in Larry McMurtry's *The Last Picture Show*, a novel and later a movie about a dying West Texas town and the younger residents who try to grasp a future that will be vastly different from that of their parents. Up and down the Carolina Piedmont textile region, for example, in such places as China Grove, Ware Shoals, and Pelzer, the theater is closing. All of these are one-industry towns brought to life by textiles in the late nineteenth century, only to be smothered by foreign competition, mechanization, and corporate mergers late in the twentieth.

The closing of the mill meant the closing of the town. In 1906 the Riegel Textile Corporation created Ware Shoals, South Carolina, on the banks of the Saluda River. At the end of 1984 the company shut down its plant, throwing nine hundred people out of work. The younger people moved elsewhere to find work, leaving a town in which 60 percent of the population is retired. Riegel had provided 60 percent of the tax base and 20 percent of the school budget. Mayor Hugh Frederick tried to put a brave face on the situation: "Riegel built the town. They built all the homes around the mill. They provided the water, electricity and the company store. It looks bad, but we've got a lot of assets. . . . We're pretty gritty people."

In other Piedmont communities, death did not come so suddenly, but the long decline has set in. Vacant storefronts dot downtown Chester, South Carolina. In Whitmire, South Carolina, after textile giant J. P. Stevens cut its work force, a department store, a drugstore, and a clothing store left the downtown. Beauty shops and churches remain, but the young people leave.

Even in the metropolitan South, shadows filter through the sunlight. The oil glut has produced real-estate and savings-and-loan fiascoes in Texas and Louisiana cities. Most new jobs are at the lower end of the pay scale, such as flipping hamburgers and cleaning hotel rooms. The service economy has created a two-tiered work force, with the highly educated, white-collar workers coming mainly from the North and the poorly paid, unskilled workers from the South. As early as 1974, Edward D. Smith, chairman of First National Bank of Atlanta, noted: "You can go to any gathering of businessmen in Atlanta, and I'll bet you five dollars to a ginger cake that at least fifty percent of them will not be natives."

Today some of these businessmen are likely to be from abroad. The South led the nation in foreign investment during the 1980s. There is scarcely a medium-sized city in the South without some ethnic diversity, as measured by the produce on supermarket shelves, the dialects heard at the shopping malls, and the English-language programs in the schools. The Sunbelt economy has attracted new immigrants from Southeast Asia and Latin America in much the same way that the North attracted an earlier wave of immigration. The average worker could care less whether his or her paycheck comes from Tokyo or Tupelo, but if there is an economic crunch, Tupelo will feel it first and foremost. In 1971, Mississippi businessman Stewart Gammill III saw the coming trend and wondered what impact foreign-owned firms would have on the South, considering that, historically, businesses coming into the region "have, through the years, had little if any concern for the natural resources, the level of education, or the quality of life in the South. On the contrary, it has been in their interest to maintain a low level of achievement and limited political awareness among both blacks and whites. To have it otherwise would directly threaten long-term profits and growth potential."

Concern over the quality of life is intimately connected with Southern economic development because recruiters promote the region's environment as a major attraction. Ironically, the very success of recruiters' efforts has threatened that selling point. Paper mills in the Savannah area, nuclear waste in rural Alabama, chemical factories in the Richmond region, land development in marshlands and along the coast, petrochemical industries in Louisiana, and increased auto exhaust almost everywhere have jeopardized the natural South. State environmental legislation passed in the 1970s and early 1980s, as well as the emergence of limited-growth advocates in various localities, are beginning to curb the most serious polluters, though the traditional fear of ruining a good business climate tends to dominate the concern over ruining a good environment.

In the past, the South has not been able to afford the luxury of thinking about environmental issues. Now it must, not only for the sake of the environment, but also for its future economic welfare. Quality-of-life issues are becoming increasingly important to service-industry executives, and the national competition for their business is fierce. The highly publicized Sunbelt/ Frostbelt split is irrelevant today. By the mid-1980s, the erstwhile economic basket cases of the Northeast and Midwest had experienced a remarkable (at least to experts) resurrection. States like Maine, Massachusetts, and Ohio turned up on most-likely-to-succeed lists in terms of creating new jobs by the year 2000. Magazines touted Pittsburgh and Baltimore as "most livable cities." Even Cleveland began to get some positive press notices.

One important reason for this seeming turnaround is that, through the difficult transition from an industrial to a service economy, the Northern states retained some of the basic building blocks for economic development, particularly a fine educational system. In Massachusetts, for example, more than half of the 2,000 Ph.D.'s produced each year stay in the state. MIT graduates alone have started more than 1,000 businesses since 1970.

The university has become an important partner for economic development, and North Carolina's Research Triangle Park was an early indicator of that trend. The South has some excellent universities, but its secondary and primary schools lag behind those of other regions. When no Southern state can equal the national average for teachers' salaries, and when one out of three adult Southerners lacks a high school degree, the South becomes less attractive to service-economy businesses. As former Tennessee governor and now president of the University of Tennessee Lamar Alexander observed, "If 90 percent of the people have a high school education in Minneapolis and 67 percent do in Tennessee, we're not going to be able to keep up, much less catch up."

In other words, in order to maintain the pace of economic development and compete successfully in the national and international economies, Southern recruiters will need to recast their message and Southern states will need to follow through on environmental and educational initiatives to support those efforts. The days of boosters' offering low-wage, nonunion labor and low taxes as incentives are not over. During the mid-1970s, Philip Morris hoped to locate a major cigarette plant in Concord, North Carolina, the county seat for Cabarrus County (within the Charlotte metropolitan area). At that time Cannon Mills dominated the employment base of the town and surrounding county (and the politics as well). As one Cannon employee noted, "Mr. Charlie [Cannon] don't want nobody coming in here and running up wages," and the Philip Morris facility presented the double threat of a unionized work force that was paid a dollar per hour more than the prevailing industrial wage in the county. Cabarrus County also happened to be, not coincidentally, the least unionized industrial county in the United States. Philip Morris eventually located its facility outside Concord but within the county. A recommendation to offer an official "Welcome to Cabarrus County" greeting from the chamber of commerce ended in a tie vote. The cigarette manufacturer had experienced a rough odyssey through the Piedmont; it had sought Greenville, South Carolina, as an alternate site only to run into the sentiment expressed by a local construction company executive, "Let's run those bastards off."

On occasion these obstructionist tactics were evident even in some of the Piedmont's larger urban centers. In 1974 the Raleigh Chamber of Commerce attempted to block the Xerox Corporation from locating a unionized facility near the city. The company's wage scale was twice the state average. At the same time, the chamber was promoting a referendum to approve industrial development bonds so that North Carolina would be able "to compete with neighboring states for blue-chip, high-wage industry." A few years later, the chamber flexed its muscles again, running out the Miller Brewing Company, a firm similarly known for high wages and union labor. Journalist Marshall Frady claimed that "the devout acquisition of factories became a kind of second religion" in the South. But some places observed strict adherence to denominational lines.

By the late 1980s, as national competition heated up, there were fewer examples of such behavior, though older economic ideals persisted. In June 1989, a *Charlotte Observer* headline blared, "Manufacturing Climate Is Sunny." The *Observer* was commenting on a national survey undertaken by a Chicago firm to determine the most attractive states for manufacturing. North Carolina ranked as the fourth-best state in the nation based on a combination of five categories. The state ranked first in the category of employee costs, which meant that such basic employee benefits as unemployment compensation and worker's compensation payments were the lowest in the nation. It also rated high—tenth—on government fiscal policies (that is, taxes). On the other hand, North Carolina ranked forty-sixth nationally in the quality-of-life category. The survey defined quality of life as education, health care, cost of living, and transportation. An economic profile taken a century ago would have listed worker exploitation, low taxes, poor education, and minimal social services among the major characteristics of the state's economy. Obviously, the state's economic condition has improved significantly over the past one hundred years; relative to the rest of the nation, however, those adverse statistics not only persist but community leaders are proud of them.

These shadows over the Sunbelt should not obscure the remarkable economic transformation that has occurred in the South since World War II: from the nation's poorest region to its wealthiest; from the leading exporter of people to the prime destination for Northern and foreign newcomers; and from an economy dependent on staple agriculture and low-wage industry to a diverse, service-oriented economy. If some past vices persist, so do some virtues—including the strong sense of past and place and, above all, civility. Can the South hold on to these virtues as it continues to mature economically? The South has withstood great changes—war, poverty, and out-migration, to name just a few—and has remained the South. Chances are it will continue to blend the new prosperity with the old culture, just as many of its newcomers have been lured and secured by the Southern lifestyle. At the least the possibilities exist. Bob Hall, editor of *Southern Exposure* magazine (and more prone to point out the region's shortcomings than to blindly herald its attributes), notes, "There's nothing pure about the South, but the possibilities that the South offers for us are a lot better than the possibilities in a lot of other places. Because the possibilities in the other places have been eliminated, rooted out."

JULIA KIRK BLACKWELDER is a native of Saratoga County, New York. She received her undergraduate training in American civilization at the University of Pennsylvania in 1964 and soon thereafter departed for Atlanta to seek another civilization. After receiving her Ph.D. from Emory University in 1972, she remained in Atlanta for several years. In 1976 she moved to the University of North Carolina at Charlotte, where she is now chair and professor of history. She has written a variety of books and articles on topics relating to the experience of women in the South, most notably *Women of the Depression: Caste and Culture in San Antonio, 1919–1939*. She is currently working on a study of female labor and family life in twentieth-century America—a book that will include at least a Southern dimension.

PAUL D. ESCOTT was born in St. Louis, Missouri, and lived in Massachusetts and Vermont before coming to North Carolina in 1971. For years now he has been calling himself a Southerner. Educated at Harvard University (B.A.) and Duke University (M.A. and Ph.D.), he taught at the University of North Carolina at Charlotte for many years before moving to Wake Forest University, where he is Reynolds Professor of History. His publications include *After Secession: Jefferson Davis and the Failure of Confederate Nationalism; Slavery Remembered: A Record of Twentieth-Century Slave Narratives; Many Excellent People: Power and Privilege in North Carolina, 1850–1900*; and, with coeditors Jeffrey Crow and Charles L. Flynn, Jr., *Race, Class, and Politics in Southern History*.

DAVID R. GOLDFIELD was raised in Brooklyn, New York, and educated at Brooklyn College (B.A.) and the University of Maryland (M.A., Ph.D.). In the mid-1960s he made his first extended foray into the South, fell in love with the region, and by 1970 had settled in Birmingham as a permanent resident. He has taught at Birmingham-Southern College, Virginia Polytechnic Institute, and, for the past nine years, at the University of North Carolina at Charlotte, where he is Robert Lee Bailey Professor of History. He is the author of *Cotton Fields and Sky-scrapers: Southern City and Region*; *Promised Land: The South since 1945*; and, most recently, *Black, White, and Southern: Race Relations and Southern Culture, 1940 to the Present*. Goldfield also serves as a consultant for history museums in several Southern cities.

NELL IRVIN PAINTER is from Oakland, California, where her parents took refuge from the Jim Crow South during World War II. After a scattered education that ended with a Ph.D. in American history at Harvard University, she served a lengthy Southern apprenticeship teaching at the University of North Carolina at Chapel Hill. Currently she teaches the history of the South at what used to be called the Southern-most Northern college in the country, Princeton University. She is the author of *Exodusters: Black Migration to Kansas After Reconstruction; The Narrative of Hosea Hudson: His Life as a Negro Communist in the South;* and *Standing at Armageddon: The United States, 1877–1919*. Currently she is working on a study of sexuality in the nineteenth- and twentieth-century South and a biography of the Northern antislavery and women's rights reformer Sojourner Truth.

JOHN SHELTON REED was raised in Tennessee and educated at the Massachusetts Institute of Technology and Columbia University.

Since 1969 he has been at the University of North Carolina at Chapel Hill, where he is William Rand Kenan, Jr., Professor of Sociology and director of the Institute for Research in Social Science. His books include *The Enduring South*; *Southern Folk, Plain and Fancy*; and *Whistling Dixie: Dispatches from the South*. In addition, he has served as president of the Southern Sociological Society and has lectured on the South at over eighty colleges and universities in the United States and abroad.

THOMAS E. TERRILL was introduced to the wonders of country ham, redeye gravy, grits, and biscuits at his future wife's North Carolina home. In 1966, after Terrill finished his Ph.D. in history at the University of Wisconsin, he headed south to join the faculty of the University of South Carolina. There he taught the first black history course ever offered in a previously all-white university in the South. His scholarly works include books, articles, films, and video, some of which have been telecast nationally. He served as chief academic consultant for "The American South Comes of Age," a video series. Terrill is a coauthor of the recent *The American South: A History*, the first new comprehensive history of the South to be published in forty years.